# Angels Unveiled

## A Sufi Perspective

Second Edition

Shaykh Muhammad Hisham Kabbani

*By those that winnow with a winnowing*
*And those that bear the burdn of the rain*
*And those that glide with ease upon the sea*
*And those who distribute blessings by command,*
*Lo! That wherewith you are addressed is indeed true! (Quran 51:1-5)*

# Angels Unveiled

## A Sufi Perspective

Second Edition

Shaykh Muhammad Hisham Kabbani

Preface by Sachiko Murata

Institute for Spiritual and Cultural Advancement

ISBN: 978-1-930409-74-3
This book was first published as *Angels Unveiled: A Sufi Perspective.*


Cover and Illustrations by
**Rukkiah Tonette Sazonoff**

**Library of Congress Cataloging-in-Publication Data**
Kabbani, Shaykh Muhammad Hisham.
Angels unveiled: A Sufi Perspective

Includes bibliographical references.
1. Sufism. 2. Islamic Belief. I. Kabbani, Shaykh Muhammad Hisham.
II. Title.
BP1898.N38 1995
297'.4--dc20
ISBN 1-56744-514-4

96161283

Published and distributed by:
**Institute for Spiritual and Cultural Advancement**
17195 Silver Parkway, #401
Fenton, MI 48430 USA
Tel: (888) 278-6624
Fax: (810) 815-0518
Email: staff@naqshbandi.org
Web: www.naqshbandi.org

This book can be purchased via the Internet at: www.isn1.net

To my master,
Shaykh Muhammad Nazim Adil al-Qubrusi
an-Naqshbandi al-Haqqani
and to my wife, his daughter,
Naziha

# Contents

# About the Author

The author at a conference in Seville, Spain.

Shaykh Muhammad Hisham Kabbani is a world-renowned author and religious scholar. He has devoted his life to the promotion of the traditional Islamic principles of peace, tolerance, love, compassion and brotherhood, while opposing extremism in all its forms. The shaykh is a member of a respected family of traditional Islamic scholars, which includes the former head of the Association of Muslim Scholars of Lebanon and the present Grand Mufti[1] of Lebanon.

---

[1] Arabic: *mufti*—The highest Islamic religious authority in the country.

In the U.S., Shaykh Kabbani serves as Chairman, Islamic Supreme Council of America; Founder, Naqshbandi Sufi Order of America; Advisor, World Organization for Resource Development and Education; Chairman, As-Sunnah Foundation of America; Chairman, Kamilat Muslim Women's Organization; and, Founder and President, The Muslim Magazine.

Shaykh Kabbani is highly trained, both as a Western scientist and as a classical Islamic scholar. He received a bachelor's degree in chemistry and studied medicine. In addition, he also holds a degree in Islamic Divine Law, and under the tutelage of Shaykh Abd Allah Daghestani license to teach, guide and counsel religious students in Islamic spirituality from Shaykh Muhammad Nazim Adil al-Qubrusi al-Haqqani an-Naqshbandi, the world leader of the Naqshbandi-Haqqani Sufi Order.

His books include: *Illuminations* (2007), *Universe Rising* (2007), *Symphony of Remembrance* (2007), *A Spiritual Commentary on the Chapter of Sincerity* (2006), *Sufi Science of Self-Realization* (Fons Vitae, 2005), *Keys to the Divine Kingdom* (2005); *Classical Islam and the Naqshbandi Sufi Order* (2004); *The Naqshbandi Sufi Tradition Guidebook* (2004); *The Approach of Armageddon? An Islamic Perspective* (2003); *Encyclopedia of Muhammad's Women Companions and the Traditions They Related* (1998, with Dr. Laleh Bakhtiar); *Encyclopedia of Islamic Doctrine* (7 vols. 1998); *Angels Unveiled* (1995 first edition); *The Naqshbandi Sufi Way* (1995); *Remembrance of God Liturgy of the Sufi Naqshbandi Masters* (1994).

In his long-standing endeavor to promote better understanding of classical Islam, Shaykh Kabbani has hosted two international conferences in the United States, both of which drew scholars from throughout the Muslim world. As a resounding voice for traditional Islam, his counsel is sought by journalists, academics and government leaders.

Exordium

*When Hell was created,*
*the hearts of angels flew away*
*from their proper places.*
*When human beings were created*
*those hearts came back.*

All Praise be to God Who has inspired us with the wonderful signs of His creation and granted us the goodness of His knowledge and love by sending us His Messengers, showing us His truths, both the manifest and the hidden. Praise be to God Who has allowed us to peer into His hidden treasures, Who alone adorned Himself with His divine attributes before languages came to be, and Who is alone in the uppermost stations of Beauty and Majesty where all seekers are drawn and hope to reach. There lovers chant and dance in His remembrance with burning love, there sincere servants seek His pleasure as Messengers from His divine presence. He is the First to be worshipped, without beginning. He is the Everlasting without end. He is the King Who alone creates and invents. He is the Owner and Ruler of His kingdom both seen and unseen, angels and human beings. He is the Master Whom none resembles, ever besought and in need of none. Nothing can contain Him and He contains everything. He is the Self-Subsistent Who sustains the seven earths and the seven heavens and all universes with His power. He is unique in His perfect attributes. He is the Living, the Everlasting, Whose life knows no end. He is the Knower in His ancient knowledge. He is the Expert in creation, the All-Encompassing in both hidden and manifest knowledge. He is the Witness before Himself of His own Oneness. He is the All-Hearing without necessity to listen. He is the All-Seeing without necessity to look, the Watchful Who overlooks nothing concerning His angels and His servants. He is the Preserver Who never forgets, the Guardian of His creation, the All-Powerful of old Who brought an unlimited creation into existence. He is the Provider of all without being asked. He is the Light of lights with which the hearts of His believers are enlightened. His Kingdom no more diminishes in the wake of His generosity than an endless ocean whose waves keep breaking upon the shore.

# Preface

Islam as a religion cannot be understood without angels. The Arabic word for angel, *malak*, means messenger, and according to Islamic belief, God has entrusted His angels with every sort of divine message in the broadest sense of the term. Through these "messages" He carries out His activities in the universe. For example, it is said that an angel accompanies every drop of rain, and that seven angels are needed for a leaf to grow on a tree. From the very beginning of the creation of human beings, and even long before—angels played important roles in the universe. When God decided to create Adam, He ordered an angel to bring back a handful of soil from the earth, and then He kneaded and shaped the soil with His own two hands. After God gave life to Adam's clay by breathing into it something of His own spirit, He commanded the angels to bow down before Adam. God provides guidance for people during their life in this world through the prophetic messages and these messages in turn were brought to the prophets by the angels. Thus the archangel Gabriel was sent to Mary with God's word, Jesus, and he was also sent to the Prophet Muhammad with the Quran. And just as Gabriel brought God's word down to Muhammad, so also he was Muhammad's guide on his night journey (*miraj*) back to God.

These teachings certainly suggest that the angels are the means whereby God reveals the theoretical framework for a good and wholesome life, and also the means whereby He provides the intimate, luminous guidance through which people move toward Him on their own "night journeys." When people reach the end of their allotted lifetimes, God sends Azrail, the angel of death, to take their souls. When they enter the grave, they are visited on the first night by two angels, Nakir and Munkar, who ask about their beliefs and activities in this world. Throughout the life of each person, two angels are in charge of recording his or her conduct, and the scrolls that they write become decisive documents on the Day of Judgment.

It is said that angels are created from light, human beings from water and earth, and the jinn from fire. The human spirit (*ruh*) is a divine breath that is blown into the body, thus giving life to earth and water. According to Islamic cosmological teachings, a human being is made of spirit, soul, and body, or light, fire, and clay. Spirit is a luminous and intelligible substance akin to the angels and thus we can say that all human beings carry an angelic nature in themselves. The soul is the sum total of the human faculties that are situated between light and darkness, or spirit and body, and this is the domain of "fire" from which the jinn were created. This helps explain why the Prophet said that Satan, who is an evil jinn, runs in the blood of every human being.

Islam's confession of faith begins with an assertion of tawhid, the Unity of God. But the Quranic formulas that define faith in more detail include faith not only in God and His unity, but also in God's angels, His prophets, His Books, the Last Day, and the measuring out of both good and evil. Thus faith cannot be Islamic faith if it leaves out the angels. And this has much to do with the fact that according to Islamic cosmological and psychological teachings, human beings are not truly human unless they live up to their own angelic nature—the luminous divine breath that was blown in their clay after it was kneaded and shaped by God Himself.

Angels Unveiled is a most welcome book. It provides many traditional Islamic accounts of angels in a beautiful and simple language that will be appreciated by everyone. As Shaykh Hisham Kabbani says—angels give hope to the believers. The angelic world of light is the past, the present and the future of every human being. To have hope in the future is deeply rooted in knowledge of the past, which in turn is only possible at the present moment. To live every moment in the best manner is part of the quest of all spiritual seekers. The various aspects of the angelic world that are described in this book are a great gift to all those interested in the life of the spirit, whether they be Muslim or otherwise, and Shaykh Hisham's efforts will be appreciated not only by those who read the book but also by those who do not read it but are given hope by readers who retell the stories.

Sachiko Murata<br>
Mt. Sinai, NY<br>
August, 1995

# To the Reader

Gentle Reader, I bring you the traditional greeting of peace which has been used by spiritual people all over the world: *al-salamu alaykum.*

I am very pleased to notice the growing awareness, among the general public, of the phenomenon that has come to be known as "angels." This is the sign of an awakening of belief in the vast unseen world around us, and also the awakening of a hunger to go beyond the bounds of our spiritual senses and to fulfill the unexplored potential in each one of us.

Assuredly angels do exist. They have a place in the cosmos amidst the myriad, uncountable servants of our Creator—and they play a special role in the divine plan.

Since the beginning of mankind's sojourn on this world, there have been among us people who possess a rare and precious gift: the ability to penetrate and understand some of the mysteries of this subtle universe, and to bring back for the rest of us the pearls of their wisdom and experience. These men and women are the saints and holy people that are known to every culture and civilization, and the heart of every seeker yearns to meet one of them.

I was privileged and honored in the extreme not only to meet but to accompany two such masters, great saints of the Islamic mystical tradition of the Naqshbandi Sufi Order, Shaykh Abdullah al-Daghestani of Central Asia and Shaykh Muhammad Nazim al-Haqqani of Cyprus, may God sanctify their blessed souls and raise them higher and higher in knowledge and wisdom.

Over many years and after a rigorous training, they were able to pour into my heart something of their immense knowledge and wisdom. It is my sincere wish to be able to communicate some of this experience to you, along with a small sampling of the magnificent stores of wisdom about the angelic world that are contained in our

Sufi tradition. I hope you will find the adventure worthwhile and that you, dear reader, can take encouragement to journey further.

Shaykh Muhammad Hisham Kabbani.

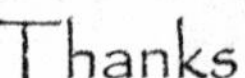

# Thanks

My special gratitude goes to Dr. Gabriel Haddad for his proper devotion, Dr. Laleh Bakhtiar and Liaquat Ali of KAZI Publications, and many others followers of the most distinguished Naqshbandi Sufi Order.

# Introduction

What
Are
Angels?

*Angels are the hope of humanity. They are the source of light*
*and the energy of creation. They are the beacons for every seeker,*
*the oasis in every desert,*
*the waves in every ocean,*
*the spring of every river,*
*the crystal in every diamond. They are*
*the dew from heaven on every leaf. They are*
*the life in every drop of blood in animate beings,*
*the motion behind every living cell. They are*
*the driving force of constellations*
*and galaxies.*
*They are the stars*
*and suns*
*and moons in every firmament.*
*The universes swim in their orbits. They are the superpowers known*
*by all traditions, beliefs,*
*and philosophies.*

It is universally known, based on these sources, that God created the angels to carry out His orders and transmit the messages that pertain to human beings. Angels are honored, subtle beings created from light who serve their Lord. They exemplify the qualities of perfection, obedience, and dedication. They can take any form they like at any time and place. They carry unlimited miraculous powers through which they can reach anyone in the blink of an eye to help and to heal, to serve and to console, to love and to be loved.

Angels take any form they wish in the physical world. As crystal water takes the form of the cup in which it is poured, angels can take the form of any creation which they visit. They do not retain their full original form of light when they are sent to human beings:

> *Say: "If there were in the earth angels walking secure, We had sent down for them from heaven an angel [without change] as messenger"*[2]

---

[2] Surat al-Isra, 17:95

Angels can come as birds, as human beings, or as a form of light like a rainbow adorning the sky. They have a mind and a heart, but no will and no desire other than to serve and obey God. They are never too proud to obey Him.

Angels worship day and night without fatigue. They do not need to sleep, as their eyes never tire. They know no heedlessness. Their attention never wavers. Their food is glorification of God, their drink is to sanctify and to magnify Him. Their intimacy is in calling their Lord through hymning and singing His praise. Their enjoyment is to serve Him. They are devoid of any and all physiological restraints. They suffer no mood-changes.

Angels inhabit Paradise and the seven heavens. They worship more than human beings because they came before them and they have greater and more powerful faculties than they. They are more pious than human beings because they are innocent and unable to fall into mistakes or wrongdoings. They never ask forgiveness for themselves but always for human beings. This shows us how much they care for us and to what extent God created them to look after us. God made them our guardians because a guardian is more perfect than the one he guards.

## Intellectual Knowledge

Angels are more knowledgeable than human beings. The teacher, again, is better than the student. Their knowledge is of two kinds: intellectual and traditional. "Intellectual" means here: "of the essence of reality" or "of the heart." "Traditional" means: "revealed and translated down from above."

Intellectual knowledge is a must, such as knowledge about God and His attributes. It is impossible for angels, the prophets, and pious people to fail to possess it. They have no excuse in failing to know it. The knowledge that is not obligatory is the way in which God has created the wonders of creation, such as knowledge of the Throne, of the Pen, of Paradise, Hell and Heavens. In addition there is the knowledge of the different kinds of angels, human beings, the inhabitants of the earth on the ground, under the ground, in the air, and under the sea. In the latter kind of knowledge angels are undoubtedly more versed than human beings. This is because they were created long before them: angels accompanied the entire process of creation of the universes as well as that of human beings. They are also more familiar with that knowledge because of their God-given vision and hearing. But such knowledge is only attainable to those who have purified their heart and vision among human beings.

## Traditional Knowledge

As for traditional knowledge, it is the prophetic knowledge that cannot be known by human beings without benefit of revelation. Only angels are able to bring that kind of knowledge to them. They were indeed the intermediary between God and human beings in that respect. Furthermore, it is possible that they are the continuous intermediaries of the events of the Last Day, after having been those of past and present events up to the Last Prophet, Muhammad, Peace be upon him. They are knowledgeable in the traditions that particularly regard them and with which God has entrusted them. That is the reason why angels are far more knowledgeable than human beings and carry six kinds of perfect attributes:

- They are messengers from the divine presence;
- They are noble in God's sight;
- They have been empowered by God with a power rendering them capable of pure obedience;
- They are well-regarded and firmly established in the Divine Presence;
- They are obeyed in the earthly world;
- They are trustworthy in receiving, keeping, and delivering the revelation.

## Human Perfection

The perfect state of human beings can no doubt never be achieved until the angelic power is linked with it. By God's permission, angels monopolize that angelic power which enlightens any human individual that connects with it. The perfection of human beings, therefore, depends on the capacity to annihilate the human soul in the crucible of the angels. The conclusion of this process is described in the Quranic verse:

*O thou soul in complete rest and satisfaction! Return unto thy Lord, accepted and accepting! Enter thou among my servants (angels), and enter thou my Garden!*[3]

According to that verse, God causes the spirit of human beings to enter the throng of the angels first, then Paradise. A condition of entering Paradise is to receive angelic greetings and revelation, at which time one enters it as a spirit endowed with angelic attributes. God then makes of such spirits messengers for His continuous creations; they are granted the happiness of living in Paradise and enjoying the sight of their Lord. God made the greetings of angels necessary for human beings when their spirits enter into the angelic power. This is to elevate them to a higher state and produce for them a great happiness. Therefore, without the heavenly input of angels, the spirit of human beings cannot reach everlasting happiness.

The contribution of the angels to human happiness is derived from their perfection. Angels are free from any kind of anger, illusion, imagination, or delusion. This characteristic gives them the power to be in the divine presence and under God's divine light. It is because of these shortcomings that human beings are prevented from being in the divine presence. Because perfection resides only in the state of reaching the divine presence, only angels can properly be said to have the attribute of perfection among created beings.

[3] Surat al-Fajr, 89:27-30

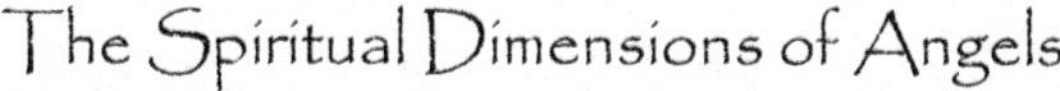

## The Spiritual Dimensions of Angels

The spiritual dimensions of angels have different aspects. The angel is a sublime luminescence. His knowledge is perfect and complete because he knows the secret of the unseen and is acquainted with the hidden secrets of creation. His knowledge is real, active, and continuous. The action of the angel is genuine because angels are committed to serve and their commitment is perfectly carried through.

Angels inhabit the seven moving planets, the polestar, and all the fixed stars of every other galaxy. Orbits are like their bodies whose hearts are the planets. The movements of these planets in their orbits is the principle of the changes on this planet earth. The movements of angels in this universe has an influence on the states of human beings on this earth. From the movements of these angels, by God's order, the connection is made between the movements of galaxies. The transmission of signals even millions of light-years away from us affect the states of human nature. The heavenly world thus always holds sway over the earthly world.

Everything is created in hierarchies and everything is connected to what is above it. Human beings always look up, not down. The desire for betterment is built into them at both the material and the spiritual levels. Everything in creation always looks up to that model. The principle of the heavenly influences is founded upon this: the effect of the upward on the downward and the aspiration of the downward to the upward.

## Angelic Light

God created the sun from the angelic light. It allows this world to see everything of the material objects that were previously wrapped in darkness. Without that light of the sun nothing can be seen. The result of the creation of light is the formation of day and night. Yet the sun is always shining day and night and its light never extinguished. Because the earth turns on its axis the changes are felt between the two states. The earth makes the sunlight appear to be extinguished. Similarly, angelic power always shines upon the earth. But the revolution of human beings around their desires create a day and a night in their heart: one side shines and the other is in darkness.

Since the moon has no light of its own, it takes its light from the sun. The latter always shines and reflects on the moon like a mirror so that it appears like a shining body. In the same way human beings, though they are inscribed by an angelic power, darken themselves through the oppression of their ego. Nevertheless, they are in a position to be always shining, and shining far more radiantly than the moon.

The moon possesses nothing of the light of the sun by itself; it only reflects at best. The main power belongs to the sun. Similarly, God has placed and organized in every orbit of the heavens, skies, galaxies, planets, and Paradises a creation differing from one orbit to another. They act like mirrors that reflect the light of the angels from the divine presence. These celestial phenomena extend that angelic light, mirror-like, for the benefit of human beings and other creations. That light is "made subject" (*musakhkhara*) to whatever is needed by creation. That light is the source of the angelic power, the very angelic power itself. Indeed, it is the substance of goodness and benefits every place of creation.

As the angels move in the divine presence, their lights move in and upon the orbits which God created to be governed by them.

Angelic powers affect the movements and contents of these orbits. Since these orbits reflect angelic lights upon earth, we see how human beings can in turn be affected by the movements of orbits in their lives. Angelic lights also affect feelings, moods, manners, and actions.

## Spiritual Clothing

The elements and qualities of human beings and other created objects on earth vary according to their respective distances from the sources of angelic power. Hence we find differences between human beings, even though their bodies are similar. This is because they differ in respect to their connections with angels. The differences are not really in bodies but in the human beings' spiritual attributes and characteristics.

Human beings carry from childhood either the characteristics of goodness and holiness, or those of evil and wrongdoing. That is a very real picture of the spiritual "dress" of human beings and their hierarchies: one receives an angelic power while the other does not. This is what makes one better than the other, just as diamonds excel emeralds, which are better than sapphire, which is better than rubies. All these are rare jewels but they vary in excellence. For all these jewels are more precious than gold. Gold is more precious than silver and silver is more precious than iron. The latter ends up as scrap while the others are always kept as valuable elements.

Light is better than darkness. The transparent is better than the opaque. The subtle is better than the dense. The enlightened person is better than the one in darkness. The beautiful is better than the ugly. The one calling to goodness is better than the one calling to

evil. The shy, courageous, generous, patient one is better than the one who carries hatred, enmity, darkness, evil, greed, and stinginess. All the above-mentioned characteristics depend on the nearness or farness of their respective bearers to the sources of angelic power.

Therefore, in this world the human spirit is a sign pointing dimly to the perfection of the higher world. It is like the light of the candle in relation to the light of the sun, or a small drop in relation to the ocean. Angelic light is the means of visibility of light on earth, both material and spiritual. We know about the sun from its rays. Similarly, we know about God from the creations of the heavens and the earth, the perception of which is brought about by the shining of angelic light upon them and their expression through revelation by that light. There is no darkness for us deeper than the non-existence of angelic light. There is no light of God more expressive for us than the angelic light. The appearance of each single thing is the result of this light, just as the existence of each thing proceeds from its existence. In this way God preserves creation through the light of the angels.

Another way to describe the way the human spirit signifies the heavenly world is through the analogy of the solar eclipse. If a portion of the sun is eclipsed you can see the sun in a cupful of water. The veil of the eclipse is the angelic light. It makes possible the appearance of the source of light. Human beings are themselves like a veil or eclipse of the angelic light. That is, they eclipse the angelic light which eclipses the light of God. Thus you can see the attributes of the Creator through His wonderful creations. This is the meaning of the Prophet's saying: *"Think of the creations of God. Do not think of His essence."*

The spirits of human beings can be described as atoms inside the heavenly world and their bodies as the houses of their spirits. Now, the house has a state and the inhabitant of the house has a state distinct from the first state. It is clear to us that the inhabitant is more honorable than the house, for the greatness of the house depends on its inhabitant.

These human spirits are an actual part of the angelic spirits. That is why the condition of entry into Paradise for the soul of a dying person is that it be accepted into the angelic realm first, as we have said. That is also why the human spirit is qualified to receive transmission from the angelic powers, as the satellite dish is made to receive transmission from the main station.

To the extent that these individuals are connected to the angelic powers, they become undoubtedly more and more important to other human beings on earth. However, human bodies remain a compound of many different elements mixed together. The bodies of angels, on the other hand, are only made of light from the divine presence. It is important to know that this difference never goes away in the material world. That is why the angels prefer to support the spirits of the bodies of prophets. For the prophetic spirits have elevated their bodily receptacles to the point where they acquire all manners of gnosis and spiritual states. These in turn enable them to become beacons of light spreading heavenly gifts and carrying God's message to His creation. All these relations between angels and prophets, saints and pious people, obtain by God's will and His permission.

Belief
in
Angels

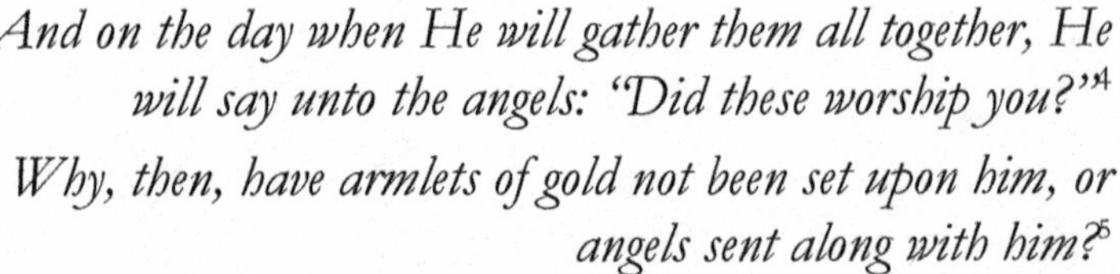

*And on the day when He will gather them all together, He will say unto the angels: 'Did these worship you?'*[4]

*Why, then, have armlets of gold not been set upon him, or angels sent along with him?*[5]

It is said that the word "angel" comes from the Latin "*angelus*," which is borrowed from the Greek "*angelos*." In Arabic the word is "*malak*" or "*malaak*," plural "*malaa'ikat*." The Arabic root verb "*alaka*," which means "to give a message," confirms the angel's etymological connection to the function of Messenger of God in the Semitic languages.

The existence of angels is one of the pillars of belief in most religious traditions and that is the case in Islam also. God mentions the angels in the Holy Quran in more than ninety different places. They also occupy prominent places in the narrations of the Prophet Muhammad, Peace be upon him, and the many accounts of saints and the pious men and women of the recent past and present. The following pages are an all-too-brief selection of some of the accounts and explanations that have reached us from those three sources.

The Quran says:

> *The Messenger believeth in that which hath been revealed unto him from his Lord and so do the believers. Each one believeth in God and His angels and His scriptures and His messengers - We make no distinction between any of His messengers - and they say: We hear, and we obey. Grant us Thy forgiveness, our Lord. Unto Thee is the journeying.*[6]

God thus orders every person to believe in His angels as an obligation parallel to that of believing in Himself, His Books, and His Messengers.

---

[4] Surah Saba, 34:40

[5] Surat az-Zukhruf, 43:53

[6] Surat al-Baqara, 2:285

## The Angels of Quran

*But God Himself testifieth concerning that which He hath revealed unto thee; in His knowledge hath He revealed it; and the Angels also testify. And God is sufficient witness.*[7]

God has created a tree in the seventh heaven, on each leaf of which is found one letter of the Holy Quran. Every leaf is a throne carved from a precious stone, and every letter is represented by an angel sitting on that throne. Every angel is the key to a different endless ocean of knowledge, which has no beginning and no end. In every ocean there is a complete universe with its own unique creation. The diver into these oceans is the Archangel Gabriel. It was he who brought to the Prophet the pearls of those oceans when he appeared to him and said three times: "Read!" To this command the Prophet, Peace be upon him, each time answered: "What am I to read?" and Gabriel said:

*Read: In the name of thy Lord who createth,*
*Createth man from a clot.*
*Read: And thy Lord is the Most Bounteous,*
*Who teacheth by the pen,*
*Teacheth man that which he knew not..*[8]

At that time the Archangel brought to the Prophet two green pieces of cloth from heaven, one of which was decorated with all kinds of precious stones from the earth, and the other with precious

---

[7] Surat an-Nisa, 4:166
[8] Surah Iqra, 96:1-5

elements from heaven. He opened the first cloth and told the Prophet to sit on it, and he handed him the second one and told him to open it. When he opened it, he received the Holy Quran with words of light, and the secret of that tree in the seventh Heaven was revealed to him. Whoever reads the Holy Quran with sincerity and piety is enabled to enter these oceans of knowledge and light. The Prophet Muhammad, Peace be upon him, saw a tablet made of rare pearls under the Throne of God and another tablet of emerald. Upon the first was the first chapter, Surat al-Fatihah, which consists of seven verses, and upon the second, the entire Quran. He asked the Archangel Gabriel, "What is the reward of one who reads the Fatihah?" Gabriel said, "The seven doors of hell will be closed for him, and the seven doors of paradise will be opened for him." The Prophet said: "What is the reward of the one who recites the whole Quran?" Gabriel replied: "For every letter that he reads God will create an angel that will plant a tree for him in paradise." Then the Prophet saw a triple light radiating in three directions, and he asked what it was. Gabriel said: "One of them is the light of the Verse of the Throne (2:255), the second is the Chapter *Ya Seen*" (Chapter 36), and the third is the Chapter of Oneness (Chapter 112). The Prophet asked: "What is the reward of one who reads the Verse of the Throne?" Gabriel replied: "God said: It is My attribute, and whoever recites it shall look at Me on Judgment Day without veil." The Prophet then asked: "What is the reward for one who reads the Chapter *Ya Seen* The answer came from God: "It consists of eighty verses, and whoever reads it will receive eighty mercies: twenty angels will bring him twenty mercies in his life, twenty more angels will bring him twenty mercies at his death, twenty more, twenty mercies in his grave, and twenty others, twenty mercies on Judgment Day." The Prophet said: "What is the reward for reading the Chapter of Oneness?" The answer came: "The angels will give him to drink from the four heavenly rivers that are mentioned in the Holy Quran: the river of pure crystal water, the river of milk, the river of wine, and the river of honey."

## Angels of the Torah

*And their Prophet said unto them: "Lo! the token of his kingdom is that there shall come unto you the ark wherein is peace of reassurance from your Lord, and a remnant of that which the house of Moses and the house of Aaron left behind, the angels bearing it. Lo! herein shall be a token for you if in truth ye are believers."*[9]

This verse shows the miraculous power of angels and their superlative ability to act upon the physical realm. They carried the Ark of the Covenant in front of Saul's army and the relics which the family of Moses and Aaron left behind. Angels were carrying the Ark of the Covenant because it was very important for humanity. It contained one of the heavenly Books, the Torah, in its original form. When God ordered Moses to write the Torah, He said: "O Moses! you have to write it on tablets of gold." When Moses asked where he would find such a metal, God sent him the Archangel Gabriel and ninety-nine other angels. Each one represented an attribute of God and they taught Moses one hundred and twenty-four thousand words. With every word Moses was elevated to a higher level. At every level Moses saw light coming to him from the Divine Presence and dressing him, until he reached a state of purity similar to the transparency of crystal water. This caused every on-looker at Moses to see nothing but light. At that moment, Gabriel ordered the ninety-nine angels to adorn him with the attributes and powers that each was carrying. Moses wore a veil to cover the intense light which emanated from him and caused others to faint if they looked at him. Then Gabriel poured into Moses' heart the heavenly knowledge meant to be consigned in the tablets. He taught him the chemistry of gold. Moses in turn taught his sister one-third of this chemistry, Joshua another third, and Saul the last third. Then he wrote the Torah on the gold he manufactured. All the while the angels stood by him and taught him how to write and adorn that heavenly book. Then God created a four-winged angel and ordered him to keep company with Moses and be the guardian of the Ark.

---

[9] Surat al-Baqara, 2:248

# The Angels of the Throne

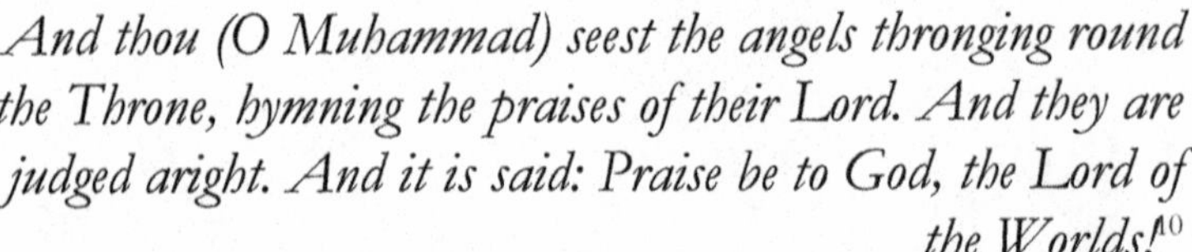

*And thou (O Muhammad) seest the angels thronging round the Throne, hymning the praises of their Lord. And they are judged aright. And it is said: Praise be to God, the Lord of the Worlds!*[10]

*And the angels will be on the sides thereof, and eight will uphold the throne of their Lord that day, above them.*[11]

God has created the Divine Throne with light from His light. The greatness of the Throne is such that, besides it, all the seven heavens and the seven earths are like a tiny mustard-seed in the midst of a great desert. When God wanted to show the greatness of the Throne, He created an angel by the name of Harquaeel. This angel has eighteen thousand wings. Delighting in his many wings, this angel was taken by the desire to appraise the size of the divine Throne. God said to that angel: "O Harquaeel, I know that you have an ambition to see the greatness of My divine Throne, so I am granting you another eighteen thousand wings, and allowing you to fly with all your might roundabout My divine Throne.

Harquaeel deployed his wings and flew for three thousand light-years until he grew tired, even though angels do not get tired, and had to rest. Again, the divine command came, saying to him: "Harquaeel, fly on!" A second time, the angel deployed his wings and flew on for another three thousand light-years. Again, he grew tired and had to stop. A third time the command came to him to fly more. And a third time he deployed his wings. He flew on another three thousand light-years until he stopped again, dazed by the great distance which not even his wings allowed him to encompass.

---

[10] Surat az-Zumar 39:75

[11] Surat al-Haqqah, 69:17

Harquaeel spoke to His Lord: "O my Lord and Creator, tell me how many times now I have circled Your Throne?" The Lord of heavens and earth and all creation answered: "O Harquaeel! you have been flying for nine thousand light-years, but you have not reached even one pillar of the base of the Throne!" Harquaeel felt shame and repented of his desire to measure the greatness of his Lord's creation and to know the extent of His secrets. God then spoke to him and said: "O Harquaeel! if I had ordered you to fly incessantly up until the Day of resurrection, you would still not be able to reach the knowledge of the first pillar of the divine Throne. No-one can know the unknowable except by My favor and My grant."

God has created eight angels to carry the divine Throne. These angels are immensely powerful and awesome. Each has a sevenfold aspect: one face in front, one face in back, one face on the right, one face on the left, one face facing up, one face facing down, and one face at the centerpoint or heart connecting all six faces. This face is the most radiant and powerful. It is the receptacle and source of angelic energy. These seven faces correspond to the seven heavens and the seven earths.

In the court of the Almighty, these angels have been granted immense honor. They are from among the very first angels to be created. The first of the eight angels has a human form and is constantly praying on behalf of the human race, saying: "O Lord! give ample provision to mankind, and look upon them with kindness and favor." The second angel is shaped like a lion, and his prayer is: "O Lord! give their provision to each animal from among the beasts of prey." The third angel is shaped like an ox and he intercedes on behalf of domestic animals and the pasturing beasts. He prays that their provision never be lacking and that they might be at ease. The fourth angel has the form of an eagle and he prays for the benefit of the birds and all winged creatures. The fifth angel is shaped like the sun and his light shines upon the planet earth. He prays for the benefit of the human race, animals, and nature, so that they may enjoy the energy that he is sending. The sixth angel is shaped like a tree whose leaves represent everything which God has created. He

prays for all these leaves that they flourish by receiving the nectar of God's praise. The seventh angel has the shape of a constellation. He is the source and the center of all the others. He turns to God and receives His light.

God placed the greatness of the divine Throne on the shoulders of these angels. Their heads are underneath the Throne and their feet reach below the seven earths. Although angels never tire, the burden of the Throne of the Almighty became too heavy for them. They were too weak to bear it. God then inspired them to praise Him in a certain way: "Glory to You, our Lord, and utmost praise! May Your Name be blessed, and Your Might, and Your Power! There is no god other than You." Then the Throne grew light on their shoulders.

God has commanded the entire host of angels in the heavens to come forward daily and give their praise to the Throne-bearers. They perform their task of praise in two shifts: one group salutes them in the morning, the other in the evening. God has ordered them to ask forgiveness on behalf of mankind. Their tears are like rivers. From every drop God creates still more angels to praise Him and to ask forgiveness for human beings until the Day of Judgment.

The angels of the Throne always bow their heads. They cannot raise up their eyes lest the light that comes from the Throne annihilate them. When the angel Harqaeel saw the greatness of the Throne and of its carriers, he recited:

*Can any sustain the Almighty?*
*A servant may carry body and soul.*
*But to carry God's Throne --*
*Who can grasp its Reality,*
*Its vastness? What eye sees the whole?*
*On no other way does eye see and word comprehend*
*Except when God says:*
*"Above His Throne exists Mercy without end."*
*Eight are its pillars,*

*Known by non but their Lord.*
*Muhammad stands first in order by right,*
*Then Ridwan, Malik, Adam columned and bright*
*Stand arrayed in rank by his side.*
*Over Gabriel, Michael, and Israfil*
*Does Abraham preside:*
*Eight veiled in darkness*
*Envision the sight:*
*How the pillars stand hid*
*In the might of their height.*

The Four
Archangels
in Charge
of the Earth

*Almost might the heavens above be rent asunder while the angels hymn the praise of their Lord and ask forgiveness for those on the earth. Lo! God is the Forgiver, the Merciful.*[12]

*And how many angels are in the heavens whose intercession availeth not save after God giveth leave to whom He chooseth and accepteth!*[13]

*A written record, attested by those who are brought near unto their Lord.*[14]

There are four angels and their innumerable retinues in charge of this world. The first is Gabriel and his armies. He is in charge of soldier-angels and revelation. Gabriel insures victory and is responsible for the extinction of nations: human, animal, vegetal, or others, when God wills it. The second is Michael and his armies, in charge of rain and vegetation. He conveys sustenance to nurture mankind. The third is "Azra'il the angel of death and his assistants. They are in charge of seizing the souls of those who die. The fourth is Israfil and his assistants, in charge of the Hour of the Day of Judgment. When the earth has passed away God will order these angels to bring forth their scrolls and they will bring them. Then God will order them to open the Book of Life. They will then find that their scrolls are the same as it.

12 Surat ash-Shura, 42:5

13 Surat an-Najm, 53:26

14 Surat al-Mutafiffin, 83:20-21

The Angel
That Carries
the Whale
That Carries
Creation

*Lo! In the creation of the heavens and the earth and in the difference of night and day are signs of His sovereignty for those possessed of understanding, such as remember God, standing, sitting, and reclining, and consider the creation of the heavens and the earth, and say: "Our Lord! Thou createdst not this in vain."*[15]

In the beginning God Almighty in His majesty created a huge jewel of green peridot. No one but He knows its size. Then the Lord trained His gaze onto that jewel and looked on it with a glance of awe. Under the influence of God's gaze, this jewel became liquid and began to undulate. It turned into a sea and began to boil and churn and was moved from its depths. As it boiled, it began to evaporate, and steam rose up from it. This vapor continued to rise, and below it remained a thickening, coagulated, precious mass. From the layers of vapor the Lord of the worlds created the seven heavens, and from the remaining primordial mass he created seven layers which He then made into the seven earths. The thickness of each of the layers of heaven and earth was five hundred thousand light-years, and as for the space separating each of them from the next only God knows it as He said:

*Have not the unbelievers then beheld*
*that the heavens and the earth*
*were a mass all sown up,*
*and then we unstitched them*
*and of water fashioned every living thing?*
*Will they not believe?*[16]

After creating the heavens and the earth, God created a great angel. Between his eyebrows there is a distance of five hundred light-years. He has two wings decorated with great constellations. They spread their lights like flickering fires over his majestic shoulders.

---

15 Surat Ali-'Imran, 3:190-191

16 Surat al-Anbiya, 21:30

One wing represents the East, the other the West. The angel was ordered to bend down his neck. With both his arms he lifted up the whole of creation spanning the East and the West. He carried this burden until he came to rest right beneath the divine Throne. There he will remain until Judgment Day.

When he lifted his burden, the angel saw that his feet remained suspended in mid-air. God then ordered the angels to bring from the highest Paradise a stone of red ruby. This heavenly rock was placed beneath the angel's feet so that he found a place for his feet. Now this red ruby remained suspended in mid-air. So the Lord brought an enormous ox which had seventy-thousand legs from Paradise. This ox was so huge that its horns reached from the highest heaven to the foot of the Divine Throne. It was immeasurably greater in size than the angel carrying the heavens and the earth. The angels placed the red ruby stone between the horns of the ox where it was firmly grounded; except there was nothing to support the feet of the ox. God, therefore, fashioned a dome-shaped vessel; its breadth was a distance of seven hundred thousand light-years. The angels placed this vessel beneath the feet of the ox. The ox now stood firm. But the vessel was left hanging in the air. From the perfection of His divine power, God created a whale by the name of Lutia. He then ordered the angels to place the vessel on its back, and the angels obeyed. By the will of God, the vessel stood fast. Now only the whale remained in the air. So God created an angel more beautiful than the new crescent moon. Half of it is fire and half snow. Its constant prayer is: "By the Lord who has made this fire cohabit in peace with this snow, may God bless and forgive His human beings." Thus God made the angel that carries the universes stand on top of the red ruby, placed on top of the ox that rested on the dome-shaped vessel that sat on the whale Lutia who swam in the palm of the angel of opposites like a ring lost in the midst of a great desert.

The
Soldier
Angels

*And when thou (Muhammad) didst say unto the believers: "Is it not sufficient for you that your Lord should support you with three thousand angels sent down to your help? Nay, but if ye persevere, and keep from evil, and the enemy attack you suddenly, your Lord will help you with five thousand angels sweeping on."*[17]

*Then God caused His piece of reassurance to descend upon him (the Prophet) and supported him with hosts ye cannot see.*[18]

*And that Our host, they verily would be the victors.*[19]

*To God belong the soldiers of heaven and earth, and God is Knower, Wise.*[20]

*Who is he that will be an army unto you to help you instead of the Beneficent?*[21]

*And none but your Lord knows the number of His soldiers.*[22]

These verses have two explanations, external and internal. In support of the righteous people who followed the Prophet Muhammad, Peace be upon him, God has ordered three thousand of the angels created from the light of the attribute "*al-Jalil,*" "The Majestic," to descend and protect the believers against terror and devils. These angels were "sent down," in other words, came down from the Seventh Heaven which is the highest heaven. The second verse shows that God has sent the angels carrying signs of special significance which were visible to the believers. These signs were crowns of gold on their head, which represent the richest and most precious state, as these angels came from the most precious

---

17 Surat Ali-'Imran, 3:124-125
18 Surat at-Tawbah, 9:40
19 Surat as-Saffat, 37:173
20 Surat al-Fath, 48:4,7
21 Surat al-Mulk, 67:20
22 Surat al-Mudaththir, 74:31

state of perfection in the first heaven. Through the light of their crowns these angels were able to strike dead whoever came in front of them. At the occurrence of that event in the battle of Badr, believers were given the power to see those angels and to believe in their support by direct sight.

The internal meaning of these verses, which very few believers experience, is based on the fact that in the Holy Quran God has ninety-nine names and attributes, whereas in the Bible He has nine hundred and one, and in the Torah, two thousand. In the first of these two verses God mentions that these angels have been sent down from the highest heaven which is in the highest state of perfection near the divine presence. Each angel was carrying one attribute of the three thousand attributes that exist in the three Holy Books. This means that holy support came from all three heavenly books and was given to the believers and their Prophet Muhammad, Peace be upon him. The symbol here is that of the unity of religion and the oneness of faith. It enabled those believers to understand that Islam accepted Jesus and Moses and the Books that they brought. The second verse defines a firm reality that egoistic devils cannot reach you as long as you are aware of God's presence in your heart. This presence elevates you to a state of perfection comprising five different levels. Each level consists of one thousand different layers or states, and each layer is represented by one of the five thousand angels mentioned. When you ascend from one level to another, you will be dressed with the power of the angel of that level. Each level increases your heart's power twofold so as to embrace all the power and knowledge of that level. This increased light provides the key to the next level, and so forth from the first to the last of the five thousand levels. At that time, you will be a light from God's Light and a deputy among His angels on earth, shining like a sun on a bright day.

PART ONE
- THE PAST

# Angels and Adam and Eve

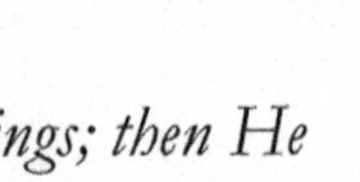

*And He taught Adam the nature of all things; then He placed them before the angels, and said: "Tell me the nature of these if ye are right."*[23]

*And behold, We said to the angels: "Bow down to Adam" and they bowed down. Not so Iblis: he refused and was haughty: He was of those who reject Faith.*[24]

*It is We Who created you and gave you shape; then We bade the angels bow down to Adam, and they bowed down; not so Iblis; He refused to be of those who bow down.*[25]

*Behold! thy Lord said to the angels: "I am about to create man, from sounding clay from mud moulded into shape; "When I have fashioned him (in due proportion) and breathed into him of My spirit, fall ye down in obeisance unto him." So the angels prostrated themselves, all of them together: Not so Iblis: he refused to be among those who prostrated themselves.*[26]

*Behold! We said to the angels: "Bow down unto Adam." They bowed down except Iblis: He said, "Shall I bow down to one whom Thou didst create from clay?"*[27]

*Behold! We said to the angels, "Bow down to Adam." They bowed down except Iblis. He was one of the Jinns, and he broke the Command of his Lord. Will ye then take him and his progeny as protectors rather than Me? And they are enemies to you! Evil would be the exchange for the wrong-doers!*[28]

---

[23] Surat al-Baqara, 2:31-33

[24] Surat al-Baqara, 2:34

[25] Surat al-ʿAraf, 7:11

[26] Surat al-Hijr, 15:28-31

[27] Surat al-Isra, 17:61

[28] Surat al-Kahf, 18:50

*When We said to the angels, "Prostrate yourselves to Adam," they prostrated themselves, but not Iblis: he refused.*[29]

*Behold, thy Lord said to the angels: "I am about to create man from clay: "When I have fashioned him (in due proportion) and breathed into him of My spirit, fall ye down in obeisance unto him." So the angels prostrated themselves, all of them together.*[30]

God taught Adam the names of everything in creation—the inner nature and the outer, qualities and quantities and the secret of all existence. It is by virtue of this knowledge that He elevated him to a state of purity and perfected him to reach the divine knowledge from which angels derive the nectar of their own knowledge. God thus enabled Adam to teach and inform the angels, although he was created after them.

These verses point to the essence of the human condition, whereby human beings can reach a station where they command angelic power. They teach us that angels can take the form of human beings, and that human beings can purify themselves to the point of carrying angelic attributes.

God has placed the angels at the service of His beloved creation, and caused them to appear to mankind and help them. This is symbolized by their prostration to Adam. It was Adam whom God chose as His viceroy on earth and not the angels.

*And had He willed He could have set among you angels to be viceroys in the earth*[31]

It is related that when Adam approached death he assembled his children and he told them that he desired to taste of the fruit of

---

[29] Surah Taha, 20:116

[30] Surah Sad, 38:71-73

[31] Surat az-Zukhruf, 43:60

paradise again. All his children went in search of such fruit. The angels knew that Adam was going to die. They received his children with heavenly shrouds in their hands and water from the rivers of paradise for Adam's final ablution. Adam's children were surprised. "How did you know that our father was ill?"

The angels replied, "What are you looking for?"

The children answered that their father was sick and that he desired a fruit of paradise. "Perhaps that will heal him," they said.

The angels told them, "O children of Adam! Paradise was created for you. We are but the caretakers of that place for you. How can the owners ask permission from the caretakers? But if you wish to enter it again, you have to come back to the divine presence and reclaim your angelic reality as before."

"How can we do that?" asked the children of Adam.

The angels replied, "You have to long earnestly to meet your Lord. He will then teach you the way back to Him."

"And then?" asked the children of Adam.

The angels said, "Then, you have to enter through the door of death."

When Adam died, the angels came down and buried him themselves, showing his children the manner of this ritual and teaching it to them for the first time. After that, the sun and the moon were eclipsed for seven days and seven nights.

## The Trial of Adam and Eve

*Then Satan whispered to them that he might manifest unto them that which was hidden from them of their shame, and he said: "Your Lord forbade you from this tree only lest ye should become angels or become of the immortals"*[32]

The inhabitants of heaven are more honorable than human beings. Adam and Eve's seduction shows that they knew this and wished to become like the angels. However, because they were also inhabitants of Paradise, and knew that obedience has to be completely for their Lord, Satan was not able to persuade them to eat from the tree. Their angelic powers were too high to blind them and they were resisting Satan's urge to disobey God. They were experiencing and feeling the taste of the heavenly life and had no inkling for something outside their grasp. When Satan saw that he could not convince them to eat from the tree, he approached them from another angle.

Adam and Even were the father and mother of humanity: God mentioned that He taught Adam all the names (as mentioned in the chapter on Adam's creation). These "names" included those of his entire posterity. Adam was carrying in his loins the totality of the seeds of his descendants. Since Satan himself carried an angelic power (he was among the angels though not an angel himself), he knew the secret of the seeds embodied in his loins. He therefore penetrated the loins of Adam and aroused in those seeds the yearning to eat of the tree and become angels, but in a deceiving way. These seeds moved the bodies of Adam and Eve to extend their hands and eat of that tree without their will. The cause of their downfall from the heavenly life to the earthly life was the action of their children.

It is impossible for an inhabitant of heaven to disobey God as they are carrying an angelic power which makes them constantly busy

---

[32] Surat al-'Araf, 7:20

with the obedience of God. It is therefore not Adam and Eve who disobeyed but their children in them. Were Adam and Eve to stay in Paradise, they would be neither disobedient nor distinguished. When they fell on earth they were yearning to their home as a person in exile or on a trip. Such yearning is the desire to be angelic and God accepted their yearning from them. He put death over them as a place of trial in order for them to know that disobedience is not accepted in Paradise. That is why death for pious people is the first sign of returning to Paradise and getting one's angelic power back so as never to repeat the mistake committed by all Adam's children in his loins another time.

It was enough suffering for all mankind to be disconnected from their angelic power for a period of time. They had to live on earth and could reach their destined states in Paradise only by means of that power. When Adam and Eve fell to earth they cried in prostration to their Lord for forty days. They were not crying for themselves but for the sake of their children and in order to protect them from heavenly punishment and minimize their difficulties and sufferings on this earth. Adam and Eve never raised their head from prostration until God spoke to them and said: "O Adam and Eve, enough! I have forgiven you and your children but I have appointed for them a short life on this earth with a delicate mixture of love and hatred, pleasure and pain, peace and conflict, beauty and ugliness, knowledge and ignorance. Whoever achieves the balance and chooses right, will be living a heavenly life on earth and will be connected with the angelic powers of Paradise. He will be a light for human beings and guide them on the right path."

# Noah's Angelic Light

*But the chieftains of his (Noah's) folk, who disbelieved, said: 'This is only a mortal like you who would make himself superior to you. Had God willed, He surely could have sent down angels. We heard not of this in the case of our fathers of old'*[33]

Noah was born with the light of prophets on his forehead. God created that light before Adam and He caused it to pass from one generation of prophets to the next until the Seal of Prophets, Muhammad.

After he received the prophecy Noah preached for nine hundred years. The angelic light in him shone forth and even the animals and stones were praising God when they saw him. Yet Noah's people were so stubborn that he succeeded in calling only eighty persons to the true faith, among them three of his sons. In the end Noah was fed up and he asked God to be relieved from the task of constantly calling in vain. God accepted Noah's request and decided to send the Great Flood as a trial for human beings. When the command came for Noah to build the ark, he asked for instructions and God sent him Gabriel to teach him how to build it.

Gabriel ordered the angels of safety to collect the best timber for a ship to resist the Waters of Wrath. The angels brought Noah a pile of wood and timber from the cedar-trees of Lebanon which were later used to build the Temple of Solomon. They placed the wood in front him. The pile was so great that from whatever point of Noah's country one looked at it, that pile always seemed to cover the sky above one's head. Noah took one splinter of that pile and from it began to build a huge ark.

Never before had a ship been built in that country. Noah's country did not meet the sea or any other great body of water. His people scoffed at him, saying: "A ship in the middle of a plain!" and:

---

[33] Surat al-Mu'minun, 23:24

"How should there be a flood in this country which hasn't even seen rain in so many years?"

Gabriel instructed Noah how to piece together the hull of the ship with one hundred and twenty-four thousand planks. On each of these planks was inscribed the name of one of the one hundred and twenty-four thousand prophets who were to appear from the beginning of creation to the end of times, starting with Adam. God created an angel to safeguard and insure the soundness of each plank even after it had been incorporated into the ship. This was done to show that God protects his creation with his beloved ones among the angels and the prophets. God places within creation itself the causes and effects of salvation and the road to Paradise. God saves His beloved servants time and again with the arks of salvation brought by the angels. In times of disasters, plights, wars, famines, and great depressions, angels never fail until today to bring help and relief for those who ask.

# Abraham's Honored Guests

*Hath the story of Abraham's honored guests reached thee (O Muhammad)?*[34]

Abraham's nickname was: "Father of guests" because he was so hospitable. Because of his great hospitality, God always sent him an angel to keep company with him, so that Abraham would not have to sit and eat alone. One time God sent Abraham three angels to bring him news of a son, although he and his wife were quite old. It is said that the three angels who visited Abraham are called "honored" because Abraham, the Intimate Friend of God, served them himself. It is also said that they are called this because the guest of an honorable person is himself honorable.

God blessed the lands of the entire Middle East with great angelic presence and light. He caused all the prophets and saints who are mentioned in His revealed Scriptures and traditions to be born there. God made them visit and bless the various locations that He caused to bathe in perpetual angelic light, such as Mecca, Madina, Jerusalem, Damascus, Sinai, Yemen, and the mountains of the Lebanon. God brought Abraham to Syria and called it:

*The land which we have blessed for the benefit of the worlds*[35]

One day Gabriel asked God: "O God! show me one of Your beloved servants." God sent him down to see Abraham. Gabriel searched the earth and found him sitting with his son on a hill overlooking a valley entirely filled with flocks of sheep and cattle. In the blink of an eye Gabriel appeared before him as a man and addressed him: "O stranger! what is your name?"

"My name is Abraham."

"And who is this with you?"

---

[34] Surat adh-Dhariyat, 51:24

[35] Surat al-Anbiya, 21:71

"My son."

"What are you doing on this hill?"

"Tending those flocks you see below."

"Whose flocks are these?"

"They are mine."

Abraham was wondering why this man was asking all these questions but he kept quiet. Gabriel went on questioning him and checking his faith. He said:

"O Abraham! These flocks are too many for you."

"They are not too many but if you would like to have a share I can give you some."

"Yes, but I cannot pay the cost."

"The price will not be too much for you but it will be dear to me."

"I do not understand."

"Ask me."

"What is the price, O Abraham?"

"The price of half this flock is under your tongue and between your lips."

"What is that?"

"It will take only a few seconds to move your tongue and your lips with some words then half the flock will be yours."

"What are these words?"

"Are you accepting my terms?"

"Yes, I accept."

"Then say: '*subbuhun quddusun rabbul mala'ikati war ruh*—Most Glorious and Holiest, Lord of the angels and the Spirit!'"

Gabriel said: "*Subbuhun quddusun rabbul mala'ikati war ruh.*"

"O my son! go down right away and put half of these flocks on the side for our guest."

Gabriel continued Abraham's examination: "O Abraham! What remains is still too many for you and your son alone, while we, my tribe and I, are greater in number than you."

"O my brother! Do not worry. I shall give you another half of the remaining half if you say a second time:Most Glorious and Holiest, Lord of the angels and the Spirit!'"

God ordered all the angels in heaven to pay attention at the dialogue between Gabriel and Abraham and to marvel at the latter's faith and loyalty. Gabriel again said: "*Subbuhun quddusun rabbul mala'ikati war ruh.*"

Abraham immediately ordered: "O my son! Take half of the remainder and add it to the first half."

Then he looked at the man and said: "I feel that you want to ask for more. I will not wait for you to ask again. I shall ask you myself if you want more."

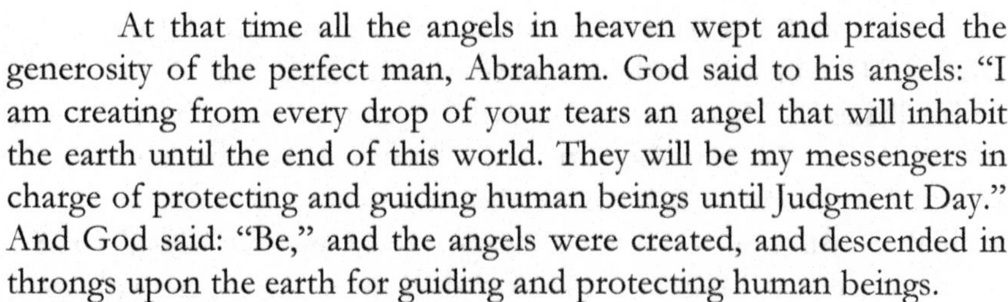

At that time all the angels in heaven wept and praised the generosity of the perfect man, Abraham. God said to his angels: "I am creating from every drop of your tears an angel that will inhabit the earth until the end of this world. They will be my messengers in charge of protecting and guiding human beings until Judgment Day." And God said: "Be," and the angels were created, and descended in throngs upon the earth for guiding and protecting human beings.

That was for one person, Abraham. What about all the other pious ones, prophets and saints who, like Abraham, are causing God's mercy to descend on the earth for our benefit?

Then Abraham said to Gabriel: "Say: 'Most Glorious, Holiest, our Lord and the Lord of angels and the Spirit!'"

Gabriel said: "*Subbuhun quddusun rabbuna wa rabbul mala'ikati war- ruh.*"

Abraham then said to his son: "O my son! Leave everything for our visitor and let us go. I have received the price I asked. These three utterances of blessing on my Lord are more precious to me than all these flocks."

"Abraham, wait!" said the visitor. "I am Gabriel the angel, I only came to check your love and your sincerity. I don't need all these flocks!"

"O Gabriel! Abraham said, did you think I did not know it was you? Were you not aware that I recognized you from the first moment you came here? You came veiling yourself from me but I pointed you out when I asked you to praise your Lord with the words: 'Lord of the angels and the Spirit.' It is I who covered myself from you. I differentiated myself from you when I made you say the third time: 'Our Lord (Lord of human beings) and the Lord of angels and the Spirit.'"

Gabriel was baffled by Abraham's answer. He did not know what to do with the cattle and sheep! God called him and said: "O Gabriel! Leave Abraham, for he will never take them back. This is because when the generous one gives he never takes back and never reminds someone of a favor he did him. I have adorned Abraham with that attribute of Mine, al-Karim: 'the Generous One,' for his love and sincerity. Direct these flocks of sheep, cows, goats, horses, donkeys, buffaloes, and camels to the jungles of this earth. Appoint over them guardian angels to look after them. My will is that these species of animals will never be extinguished from the earth because of Abraham's generosity." Gabriel assigned angels to those flocks. Wherever you go on this earth you will find generations of these animals in every part of the globe because of the blessing of Abraham's generosity.

When Nimrod desired to hurt Abraham he had a great fire built, such as had never been seen on the surface of the earth. The fire was so great that they could not approach it in order to throw in Abraham. A man told Nimrod that he had invented a special machine which he could use if he wished. That was the manjaniq or catapult. Abraham was seized, placed in it, and thrown into the fire. All that time he was saying: "My reliance is on God!" When he landed in the fire, he said: "O God, You are One in heaven and I am one on earth worshipping You." Gabriel immediately asked God for permission to go and help Abraham. God said: "If you wish you may go and ask him if he desires help." Gabriel went down and appeared before Abraham. God told all the angels to watch what would happen and listen to Abraham's answer.

Gabriel said: "O Abraham! I came to help. Do you want me to take you out of the fire?"

Abraham answered: "Does God not see His servant, O Gabriel?"

"Yes, of course, He sees everything!"

"Then let Him do as He wishes with me, O Gabriel!"

The angel of rain asked God: "Our Lord, will you let me order the rain to put out that fire?" All the animals of creation gathered and tried to put out the fire, each using the means at its disposal. Only the gecko lizard was found fanning it. But God's order to the fire itself was faster, for God had already made the fire cool and safe for Abraham. The angels praised Abraham for his absolute trust in God. The only discomfort that he suffered at that time was that he sweated a little and Gabriel wiped his sweat for him.

Then God ordered the angel of the shade to descend and make Abraham's stay a comfortable one. The angel of the shade came down and caused a huge garden to sprout instantly in the midst of the fire. A green meadow appeared in the midst of which there was a pleasant pond filled with fish and swans from Paradise. Their scales and feathers shone like silk and reflected all the colors of creation. Servants were attending Abraham, who was found under the cool shade of a willow-tree surrounded with delicious fruits and dainty dishes, and the angels engaged him in a divine conversation, during which they revealed to him the secrets of their stations and the powers God had endowed them with, giving him everything. At that time those who were outside looking in, began to wish that they, too, would be thrown into that fire with Abraham. Even his father, who previously disbelieved in him, said: "O Abraham, what a wonderful Lord your Lord is!" And his mother actually went into the fire escorted by the angels, hugged Abraham and came back out without being harmed. No-one else could approach it without feeling an intense scorching heat.

The fire burnt uncontrollably for forty days. But Abraham's garden only increased in verdure and kept expanding with the constant visitations and blessings of the angels. At that time, Abraham's fire was the most blessed spot on the entire surface of the earth, as God looked upon it with the highest favor. He ordered all the angels of creation to pay at least one visit to His Friend Abraham.

Joseph's
Angelic
Beauty

*And when she heard of their sly talk, she sent to them (the women of the city) and prepared for them a cushioned couch and gave to every one of them a knife and said to Joseph: Come out unto them! And when they saw him they exalted him and cut their hands, exclaiming: God Blameless! This is not a human being. This is no other than some gracious angel!*[36]

God created the Prophet Joseph from the light of a special beauty which He created and placed in Paradise. Joseph's prophecy was the prophecy of beauty.

The message of love that God sends in the person of His prophets is the image and representation of beauty and love in Paradise. The message conveyed to human beings from God is: "I did not leave earth without beauty and love." Prophets are the symbol of those attributes.

Out of that beauty God created Joseph and also an angel which accompanied him all his life. That angel is created from the light of the fifth Paradise. He poured on Joseph a touch of that fifth Paradise and caused ineffable light to appear on Joseph's face and to come out from his eyes, attracting and delighting on-lookers and listeners. The sound of his voice was like the humming of an angel, so that anyone who heard him would have to leave what he was doing and come and sit before him to listen to him. The ladies of the Prince's house were attracted to the angel that resembled Joseph's image and who accompanied Joseph unbeknownst to all. That experience was also a test upon Joseph to show him the way to tolerance and patience so that he would carry the burden of others' sins and prevent himself from falling into them. His beauty caused him to be thrown into prison as a preamble to a great event which God had prepared for him.

---

[36] Surah Yusuf, 12:31

*Servant of God!*
*I remember those who rememberers Me,*
*My Gardens belong to those who worship Me,*
*I visit those who miss Me*
*And exist for those who love Me.*
*A lover who loves, his word is truthful!*
*He who is intimate with his lover,*
*His action is always correct!*
*Who loves to meet Me, I will love to meet him!*

Joseph answered the angel: "Yearning and fondness have driven me to the love of God. I never hated death, as His other servants do, Because I know it is the door that leads to my Beloved."

The angel replied: "O Joseph! the signs of loving God is to give precedence to God over yourself. Not everyone who worships becomes a lover of God. To love him is to leave what God does not like. Your heart and your tongue must never cease remembering Him. O Joseph! You represent the beauty of Paradise. You must carry these three characteristics or you cannot be the one who represents it:

Prefer God's word to the word of His creatures;

Prefer His meeting to the meeting of His creatures;

Serve and help all His creatures for His sake."

The angel continued: "Your prison, O Joseph! is like the fire in the heart of a lover, burning out of control. In order to show you that the burden that you have carried from the people has been accepted by God, He has made this event the spark that ignites that fire, and opens to you the way to your Beloved." Then the angel chanted:

*"O Joseph! separation from the Beloved*
*Is better than reunion,*

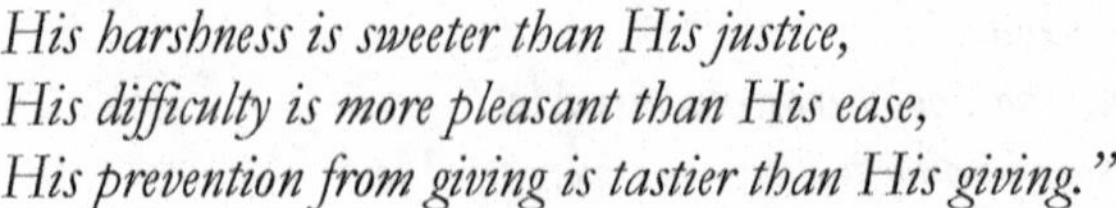

*His harshness is sweeter than His justice,*
*His difficulty is more pleasant than His ease,*
*His prevention from giving is tastier than His giving."*

Joseph said: "Explain what you mean." The angel replied: "This is because separation keeps you in a state of remembrance, for you are always yearning to reach His justice, His ease, His giving, and His taste."

The angels of Reunion-After-Separation governs the love of family members for each other, especially in times of trials and hardships. This is because God loves for human beings to keep the bonds of humanity alive between among themselves, and no earthly bonds on earth are stronger than the bonds of love: first, the love of parents for their children, which is the reflection and symbol of the love of God for His creation; second, the love of men and women for each other. The following story illustrates the contribution of angels to the reuniting of families despite the inhumane pace of modern life, which divides and separates them for materialistic reasons.

Jonah's
Angelic
Whale

*And lo! Jonah verily was of those sent to warn when he fled unto the laden ship, and then drew lots and was of those rejected; and the whale swallowed him while he was blameworthy; and had he not been one of those who glorify God he would have tarried in its belly till the day when they are raised.*[37]

God sent Jonah to the people of Nineveh in Iraq. He called them to God's message but they refused to listen to him. He was calling them night and day to no avail. Instead they harmed him and cursed him at every turn. This lasted for a long time. Jonah was unable to bear this situation any longer. He began to threaten them: "I am going to ask my Lord to send you a severe punishment which has never been seen before; to destroy your cities and burn your gardens; to make you barren and end your line." He then left them.

Slowly, his people began to feel the approach of punishment in their daily life. They began to realize that they had made a big mistake.

God is the Most Merciful; for at every moment in this world he will show His greatness and cause people to observe Him through many signs. He will do this by sending angels in order to direct the sincere, and, indeed, anyone who asks for guidance, to the light of happiness in life. God sent the people of Jonah the angels of Mercy and the angels of Safety in order to inspire their hearts to do good, and guide them to safety through the destruction that was descending on their heads.

Abraham was protected from Nimrod's fire by the intervention of the angel of snow and the angel of peace. In the immense heat of this great fire where he had been thrown, surrounded by great destruction from above, from below, and from

---

[37] Surah as-Saffat, 37:139-140

every side, Abraham was saved and protected. This was a message from God to tell His people: "I can save whomever I wish from any harm, whenever I like, no matter how bad their situation is."

Jonah was angrily moving away from his people. They regretted what they had done to their prophet. Men, women, children, old people, and even the animals, both tame and wild, were heard and seen crying out, each in his own particular language. It was a tremendous event, and everyone asked for mercy and for the angels' intercession.

God Most Merciful, Most Powerful, and Most Beneficent took away the destruction and saved them through his angels from this great havoc. Meantime, Jonah boarded a ship and took to sea. A big storm broke, and the ship was being torn apart and about to sink. The crew decided to draw lots and throw out one passenger as an expiation for the sin which was bringing death upon their heads. When they drew Jonah's lot, they loathed to throw him because he was the prophet, so they drew lots again. Every time, however, his lot kept coming out. In the end Jonah threw himself over board, and a great green whale came from the bottom of the ocean and swallowed him.

An angel appeared before the whale and instructed her not to crush Jonah but to keep him safe in her stomach. At that moment Jonah spoke to the angel and asked for his advice, saying: "Give me the glad tidings from your Lord. How did God teach you the knowledge of the Unseen?" "Because I don't commit sin," said the angel. Jonah said: "Advise me." The angel replied: "Be patient and not full of anger, for you are full of anger against your nation right now. Be a person who gives benefit, not harm -- for you were praying your Lord to destroy your people for harming you. Don't be happy with your pride and arrogance. Don't humiliate your nation with their sins, because you also have mistakes."

Inside the stomach of the green whale, Jonah went into prostration and said: "O God, I prostrated to You in a place where no one before has prostrated. O God, you have drowned me in the oceans of hope, and caused me to forget the day of my death. O Lord, you are the possessor of my heart and of my secret. I am the drowned one, so catch me by the hand and save me. Relieve me with Your perfection and inspire me with Your love! Let the angels of mercy reach down to me and pull me, O You who accept the prayers of the needy in the darkness of punishment. O Unveiler and emover of difficulties and harm, here I am coming before You, adoring You. Do not keep me from Your presence. Forgive me."

God ordered the angel to move the whale through the farthest oceans of the world and take her to the saltiest, or most concentrated and deepest depths of the seas. There Jonah began to hear the praising of all whales, all fish, all corals and all creatures of the depths. Nothing remained except they praised God and lauded Him, and Jonah was praising Him also.

[God created a saint whom he endowed with such great powers of praising and remembering that he did not need to eat or sleep. Instead, he spent all his time praying to God, chanting His Lord's praise, and making intercession for other human beings. God placed him in a room at the bottom of the ocean. There he perpetuated God's praise unhindered for hundred of years. When that saint died the angels brought him before God Who asked him: "O my beloved servant, shall I reward you according to your deeds or according to My forgiveness?" He replied: "O my Lord, according to my deeds, since you have granted that they consist solely in Your praise." The angels placed the saint's deeds on one side of the scale and on the other side they placed God's generosity to that saint. God's generosity weighed heavier, and the saint fell prostrate and speechless, begging for God's forgiveness.]

The angel inspired Jonah to say: "O God, Most Exalted, no-one can thank You nor worship You as You deserve to be thanked and worshipped. You know the secrets and the deepest knowledge, You unveil everything hidden from Your servants, You know every slight matter in this world and the next, and accept the prayer from

every creation, forgive me and accept me in Your presence as Your humble servant."

God revealed to Jonah the following:

> *And mention the Lord of the Whale Dhul-Nun, when he went off in anger and deemed that We had no power over him, but he cried out in the darkness, saying: There is no God save Thee. Be Thou glorified! Lo! I have been a wrongdoer. Then We heard his prayer and saved him from the anguish. Thus We save believers*[38]

Then God ordered the whale to throw Jonah out onto the sea-shore, and ordered the angel to tell Jonah: "This is God's mercy. He can send it on anyone He likes, even in the midst of the greatest destruction and the surest death, far from any help." Thus did God save Jonah, and the following story illustrates how God saves His people from the grip of destruction even against the greatest odds.

[38] Surat al-Anbiya, 21:87-88

Mary's
Virgin
Angels

*And when the angels said: O Mary! Lo! God hath chosen thee and made thee pure, and hath preferred thee above all the women of creation.*[39]

The "Virgin Angels" were created from the Word of God, carrying His Light and appearing to the Virgin of virgins, Mary. They informed her that she had been chosen to carry a great message for humanity. They were her guardian angels. They were wearing crowns of pearls and rubies on their head. The Virgin Mary's eyes were drawn to these pearls and emeralds without her will. This enabled her to see that this world, with all its magnitude, disappeared into one of these jewels as a ring would disappear in an ocean. This vision elevated her to a state where she attained a knowledge which dwarfed all the knowledges of this world, enabling her to carry in her womb the secret of Jesus, who is a Word from God. Through these two messengers God prepared Mary to carry the light which the Archangel Gabriel would bestow upon her at a later time and guarded her from all sorts of harm. She was asking God from her first day in existence to be a virgin in body and a virgin in soul. God granted her request, and for her sincerity and piety she was chosen, from among all the women of the world, to conceive and carry a child without the agency of a man.

[39] Surat Ali-ʿImran, 3:42

## Zachariah's Visitors

*And the angels called to him as he stood praying in the sanctuary: God giveth thee glad tidings of a son whose name is John, who cometh to confirm a word from God, lordly, chaste, a Prophet of the righteous.*[40]

The angels who came to Zachariah came as messengers, interrupting his prayer for the sake of a better heavenly communication. They told him that his wife would carry a baby of the goodly company of the righteous and that he would be a prophet. These two messenger-angels appeared to Zachariah in a purple light, showing him that they were the guardians of his baby son John who was to lead God's servants to the Right Path.

*And remember when the angels said: "O Mary! Lo! God giveth thee glad tidings of a word from Him, whose name is the Messiah, Jesus, son of Mary, illustrious in the world and the Hereafter, and one of those brought near unto God."*[41]

The guardian-messengers who came to Mary informed her that she would be carrying the long-awaited Messiah. Mary was the twenty-forth generation descendant of the Prophet Solomon whom the angels and the jinn were ordered to serve. She asked God to feed her only with lawful food that would reach her without her having to work for it since she devoted herself to His service. That is why Zachariah, her uncle, saw food by her side whenever he entered her sanctuary. When he asked from where it came she would answer from God. The two angel-messengers raised Mary from childhood to maturity without her leaving her sanctuary except to get water by a certain cave. As she was there one day she saw a large canopy of clouds filling the sky and twinkling with a variety of colors. She was fearful. Her two guardians appeared to her and said: "This is the great moment, you are going to carry your son who is going to be the

---

[40] Surat Ali-ʿImran, 3:39

[41] Surat Ali-ʿImran, 3:45

Messiah of this world." As soon as they finished, the Archangel Gabriel appeared in the image of a man dressed in white and said to her:

> *"Nay, I am the Messenger from thy Lord to announce to thee the gift of a pure son." She said: "How shall I have a son, seeing that no man touched me, and I am not unchaste?"*

The Archangel continued to say:

> *"So it will be; thy Lord sayeth: 'That is easy for me; and We wish to appoint him as a Sign unto men and a mercy from us.' It is a matter so decreed. So she conceived him, and she retired with him to a remote place."*[42]

When Mary began to feel the birthpangs at the end of her pregnancy, one of her neighbors, a carpenter named Joseph, reprimanded her with the words: "O Mary, have you seen in your life crops grow without seed?" Immediately her two guardians and Gabriel appeared to her and opened for her a vast array of knowledge. She saw nothing other than herself amidst an infinite number of angels chanting and dancing, praising and blessing and saying to her: "Say: Has not God brought out crops without seed when He created the earth?" When Joseph heard this he was struck dumb. After a while he replied to her: "You are right."

Mary was thirteen years old when she gave birth to Jesus and she died when she was 112 years old. All this while her guardian angels accompanied her and never left her. They conveyed to her God's wish to call him Jesus, the Messiah. This means in Arabic: "ʿIsa al-Masih." He was named so because he came out of the womb of his mother anointed with perfume and fragrance came from her as she was giving birth to him. From every drop of that perfume God created an angel to guard him in his life. These angels enabled him to carry the miraculous powers of healing the sick and bringing the dead

---

[42] Surah Maryam, 19:19-22

back to life. The Archangel Gabriel also anointed Jesus with his wings, protecting him from the devil. That is why Jesus in turn anointed the head of every child and orphan as a symbol of God anointing him.

Three devils approached Jesus one day. Immediately three archangels: Gabriel, Michael, and Israfil appeared. Michael blew one devil toward the east until he reached the sun and was burned by it. Israfil blew another devil to the West, until he hit the sun on the opposite side. The Archangel Gabriel took the leader and the biggest of the three, Satan, and buried him under the seven earths for seven days, insuring he did not approach Jesus another time.

*The Messiah will never scorn to be a slave unto God, nor will the favored angels. Whoso scorneth his service and is proud, all such will He assemble unto Him.*[43]

God shows that even the angels brought nearest to Him (*al-muqarrabun*) who are created from light, and Jesus who was created by a word of God through the archangel Gabriel (one of the favored angels), are happy to worship God. The implied meaning here is that God raises the angels and gives them a state like that of Jesus which means that Jesus was also one of "those brought near."

When Jesus saw the hardness of people around him he longed to meet His Lord. Angels appeared to him and supported him with the following lines:

*"O God! You made us ambitious in seeking*
*forgiveness and generosity.*
*God, You inspired us to thank You for Your favors,*
*You brought us to Your door,*
*encouraged us to look*
*what You have prepared for Your guests.*
*not all this from You,*

[43] Surat an-Nisa, 4:172

*does not all this draw us to You?*
*came to You and You brought us.*
*else than You do we desire.*
*door is vast. Its threshold is your generosity.*
*you do the poor ones reach for their goal.*
*is good for everything other than meeting You.*
*raise to you the complaint of a perplexed mind.*
*has made me drunk.*
*have forgotten the hardships of evil men.*
*know my case better than I.*
*'t leave me drunk with the wine of Your love.*
*me through Your perfect generosity.*
*own my heart. It is Your ward.*
*'t cause me to be separate from You.*
*are my secret, and I am the one drowning in it.*
*Your help and save me.*
*whom You leave behind is in disaster.*
*Your mercy is only for the good ones,*
*where will tend the hopes of sinners?*
*You Who receives the prayer of the one in need*
*the depth of a dark night,*
*You Who takes away the hardship and difficulty and pain,*
*people have slept outside of Your house,*
*You are the ever wakeful, ever-present*
*watches above all with your Mercy.*
*God! forgive those who have come against me,*
*forgive me because my love for you is pure.*
*me to your presence where I shall always see you.*

It is related that when Judas betrayed Jesus, legions of angels appeared at the side of Jesus ready to decimate the enemies of God who wished to crush His message. But Jesus stayed their hands as he was eager to let God's will come to pass and not interfere. At that time God spoke to him and said:

*Jesus, I will take thee to Me and will raise thee to Me, and I will purify thee of those who believe not.*[44]

He was taken by the angel Gabriel and raised up to heaven. On the eighth day after the crucifixion, Jesus' disciples, his mother, and another woman were gathered in Mary's house to mourn for their loss when Jesus suddenly appeared to them mysteriously. He told them the truth of what had happened and how his Lord had raised him up to the heavens where he would continue to live until the end of times when he would return to earth, and he gave them comfort.

Then he asked about Judas who had betrayed him. He was told that he had felt remorse for his betrayal, despaired, and taken his own life. Jesus said: "Ah, if only he had turned to God and begged his forgiveness, God Almighty would have pardoned him and accepted his repentence. For there is no sin great enough that our Lord in His infinite mercy would not pardon." And he wept for him.

Then he gave his disciples authority to continue preaching the Gospel and blessed them and prayed with them until dawn. The angels gathered around that holiest of meetings on earth and comforted them when the time came for Jesus to return to heaven when he was raised up again.

[44] Surat Ali-ʿImran, 3:55

Prophet
Muhammad's
Night
Journey and
Ascension

*Praise be to God Who has enraptured His servant by night from the Sacred mosque (Mecca) to the Farthest Mosque (Jerusalem).*[45]

*Lo! God and His angels shower blessings on the Prophet. O ye who believe; ask blessings on him and salute him with a worthy salutation.*[46]

*By the star when it setteth, Your companion erreth not, nor is deceived:*
*Nor doth he speak of his own desire.*
*It is naught save an inspiration that is inspired,*
*Which one of mighty powers hath taught him,*
*One vigorous; and he grew clear to view*
*When he was on the uppermost horizon.*
*Then he drew near and came down*
*Till he was distant two bows' length or even nearer,*
*And He revealed unto His slave that which He revealed.*
*The heart lied not in seeing what it saw.*
*Will ye then dispute with him concerning what he seeth?*
*And verily he saw him yet another time*
*By the lote-tree of the utmost boundary,*
*Nigh unto which is the Garden of Abode.*
*When that which shroudeth did enshroud the lote-tree,*
*The eye turned not aside nor yet was overbold.*
*Verily he saw one of the greater revelations of his Lord.*[47]

God ordered Gabriel to go down with seventy thousand angels to the Prophet Muhammad, Peace be upon him, and stand by his door. "Accompany him to My presence. And you, Michael, take the hidden knowledge and go down with seventy

---

45 Surat al-Isra, 17:1

46 Surat al-Ahzab, 33:56

47 Surat an-Najm, 53:1-18

thousand angels and stand by the door of his bedroom. You, Israfil, and you ʿAzra'il, do as Gabriel and Michael have been ordered." Then He said to Gabriel: "Increase the light of the moon with the light of the sun, and increase the light of the stars with the light of the moon." Gabriel asked: "O God, has the Day of resurrection dawned?" God said: "No, but tonight We are calling to Our presence the Prophet, the last Messenger who came after Jesus to reveal to him a secret that pertains to Us." Gabriel said: "O God, what is that secret?" God said: "O Gabriel, the secret of kings cannot be given to the servants. Go with My order and don't ask."

And Gabriel began his descent carrying with him the heavenly message. All the angels accompanied him as God had ordered, until they reached the door of the Prophet. When they arrived, they said: "*Qum ya sayyidi*: Arise, my Master, and prepare yourself! Ride on the back of the Buraq, the heavenly creature that will carry you on your journey to the Lord of Power through the land of the angels!"

## The Buraq (Heavenly Beast)

When God ordered Gabriel to carry with him the Buraq for the Prophet to ride, he went to the Paradise of buraqs and there he found forty million buraqs. Every buraq had a crown on its forehead inscribed with the words: "There is no god except God, and Muhammad is His Messenger." Under it was written: "Believe in Me, in My angels, in My holy books, and in My prophets." Gabriel saw among them a buraq who secluded himself and who sat alone crying. Gabriel came to him and asked him why he was in such a state. The Buraq answered: "I heard the name of Muhammad forty thousand years ago, and my yearning for him has prevented me from eating and drinking." Gabriel chose that buraq and he took him.

The Buraq had the body of a horse but the face of a human being, with big black eyes and soft ears. His color was that of a peacock whose plumage was set with red rubies and corals, on which sat a white head of musk on a neck of amber. His ears and shoulders were of pure white pearls attached with golden chains, each chain decorated with glittering jewels. His saddle was made of silk lined with silver and gold threads. His back was covered with green emerald and his halter was pure peridot.

The speed of the Buraq is according to his sight. His legs reach wherever his eyes can see. Gabriel said: "O Prophet, this night is your night, and your turn has come to shine in the sky of creation. You are the sun of ancient and recent knowledges; you are the moonlight of the beauties of the worlds, the happiness of creation and the adornment of the lands of human beings and angels. You are the cup of love from the river of milk and honey. The River of Kawthar in Paradise overflows in anticipation of seeing you. O Joy of all creation, O Pride of Paradise, the tables are ready and the Palaces of heaven are waiting for your coming!"

> "O Gabriel," said the Prophet, "did you come with a message of mercy or wrath?"
>
> "O Muhammad, I came with a message from your Lord to give you a secret."
>
> "What does the Lord of Generosity want to do with me?"
>
> "He wants to shower you with His mercy and all human beings that accept you."
>
> "Give me a moment to prepare myself."
>
> "I brought you water of paradise and a turban with a message enscribed: 'Muhammad the servant of God; Muhammad the prophet of God; Muhammad the beloved of God; Muhammad the Friend of God.'"
>
> "O Gabriel, tell me more about that turban."

"God created a turban from his light and he entrusted it to Ridwan, the angel-custodian of Paradise, and the praising of Ridwan's host of angels belonged to the owner of that turban before heaven and earth were created. Tonight, when the order came for your visit, Ridwan took the turban from Paradise, and all forty thousand angels said with him: 'O our Lord, you have ordered us from time immemorial to praise the owner of that turban. Honor us tonight with his sight and permit us to walk before him.' And God granted them what they asked. Then God ordered me, Gabriel, to hand Michael the precious jar of the pure water of Salsabil, and Michael to give to ʿAzra'il, and ʿAzra'il to give it to Israfil, then Israfil to Ridwan, then Ridwan sent that water another time to the Highest Paradise: Jannat al-Firdaws, where all the beautiful maiden-angels washed their faces with that water and shone even more brightly. Then they sent back that water to me, and I am giving it to you."

And the Prophet showered with the water from Paradise. As soon as it touched his noble body he became covered with a garment of subtle angelic light, and Gabriel gave him the Buraq to ride. But the Buraq stopped and asked Gabriel: "Is that the Prophet Muhammad who is invited to our Lord?" Gabriel said: "yes." The Buraq asked: "Is he the owner of the blessed pond in Paradise?" Gabriel said: "yes." The Buraq said: "Is he the leader of the People of Paradise?" Gabriel said: "yes." The Buraq said: "Is he the intercessor on Judgment-Day?" Gabriel said: "yes." At that time the Buraq began to melt like ice and snow melt in the light of the sun. He knelt down and said to the Prophet: "O Pride of creation, ride on me; but I have one request to ask of you: Do not forget me on the day of intercession."

When the Prophet began to ride he was crying. Gabriel asked him: "O Prophet, why are you crying?" He said: "I remembered human beings. Are they going to ride on Judgment Day as I am riding now on the Buraq, and go to their heavenly palaces in Paradise?" Gabriel said:

*Yes, verily, we are going to resurrect the pious ones in delegations of riders: On the Day when We shall gather the righteous unto the Beneficent, a goodly company.*[48]

At that the Prophet felt happy, and he rode forward on the Buraq. Gabriel took hold of the reins while Michael held the saddle, and Israfil the saddle-cloth. The Buraq moved in space until in the blink of an eye they reached the place appointed for their first stop in the middle of the desert. Gabriel said: "O Muhammad, go down and pray to God in this place." The Prophet said: "What is this place?" Gabriel said: "This is the place where you are going to emigrate, and it is going to be your second city." That was the town of Yathrib not far from Mecca, and its name was going to be al-Madina.

In the blink of an eye they again passed through space until they stopped a second time, and Gabriel told the Prophet to come down and pray.

"Which place is this, O Gabriel?" asked the Prophet.

"This is Sinai, where Moses used to speak with God."

Then the Buraq moved in space another time until he reached a third place where Gabriel ordered him to pray.

"And now, where are we, O Gabriel?"

"You are in Bethlehem, where Jesus was born and from where he spread the message of the King of heavens and of the earth."

As the Prophet walked with delight on the soil where Jesus was born, he felt someone moving near his right shoulder who said: "Muhammad! Wait, I want to ask you a question." But the Prophet did not respond. Then another call came from behind his left

[48] Surah Maryam, 19:85

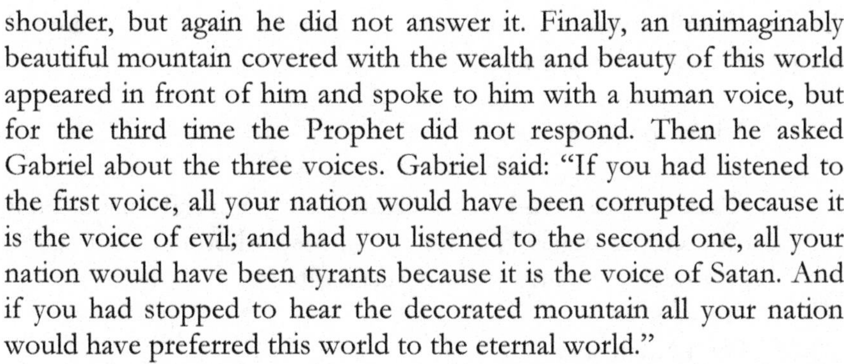

shoulder, but again he did not answer it. Finally, an unimaginably beautiful mountain covered with the wealth and beauty of this world appeared in front of him and spoke to him with a human voice, but for the third time the Prophet did not respond. Then he asked Gabriel about the three voices. Gabriel said: "If you had listened to the first voice, all your nation would have been corrupted because it is the voice of evil; and had you listened to the second one, all your nation would have been tyrants because it is the voice of Satan. And if you had stopped to hear the decorated mountain all your nation would have preferred this world to the eternal world."

The Prophet continued his way and saw two beautiful angelic beings, one masculine and one feminine. They wore a beautiful dress and the fragrance of heaven. They kissed him between his eyes and left. He asked Gabriel who these were and he said: "These are the believers of your nation. They are going to live in happiness and die in happiness and they are going to enter Paradise."

Then another angel appeared to him and offered him three cups to drink: one of water, one of milk, and one of wine. He took the cup of milk and drank, and Gabriel said: "You have chosen the cup of fitrah: innocence." Then a maiden-angel appeared and offered the Prophet three suits of cloth, one green, one white, and one black. He took the first two. Gabriel said: "White is the color of believers and green is the color of Paradise. All of your followers are going to be believers in this world and all are going to enter Paradise in the next."

Then, as the Prophet was walking on the place where Jesus taught, he entered the Temple of Solomon in Jerusalem. He found the Temple full of angels waiting for him. Every angel in the Temple represented a group of angels in paradise. Then he saw all the Prophets standing in rows. He asked Gabriel who all these were. Gabriel said: "These are your brothers from among the prophets, and these angels are the leaders of all the angels of Paradise." Then Gabriel made the call to prayer, after which he said: "O Muhammad, Most honorable of beings in the sight of God, proceed to prayer."

And the Prophet came forward and led the prescribed prayer, and all the prophets and the angels followed him.

Adam spoke saying:

"Praise be to God Who created me with His hands and ordered the angels to prostrate for me and brought out all the prophets from among my descendants!"

Then Noah said:

"Praise be to God Who accepted my prayer and saved me and my people from drowning with my ship and the help of the angels, and honored me!"

Then Abraham said:

"Praise be to God Who took me as His friend and gave me a huge kingdom, and gave me prophets for descendants, and saved me from the fire of Nimrod, and made it cool and safe for me!"

And Moses said:

"Praise be to God Who spoke to me without an intermediary and chose me for His message, and made me victorious over Pharaoh with the help of his angels, and gave me the Torah which Gabriel taught me how to write, and adorned me with His love."

And David said:

"Praise be to God Who revealed the Psalms to me, and softened the iron between my hands and all other elements, and chose me for His Message!"

And Solomon said:

"Praise be to God Who has made subject to me the winds, the jinn, and human beings; who taught me the language of birds; who gave me a kingdom which he never gave anyone after me, and supported me with all his angels."

And Jesus said:

"Praise be to God Who sent me as a Word from Him to the world, taught me the Torah and the Gospel, made me cure the deaf, the dumb, and the leper, made me bring back the dead by His permission, and supported me with Gabriel and all His angels."

And Muhammad said:

"All of you praised your Lord and I praise Him also, Who sent me as a mercy for human beings and revealed the Quran to me, expanded my breast, took out my sins, raised me up, made my Nation and all human beings the best that could be, and called me 'Kind and Merciful'"!

And Gabriel said:

"That is why, O Muhammad you are the last of Prophets and a Mercy for human beings. O prophets and angels, O creations large and small, God and His angels send blessings and salutations on His Prophet! You also send much blessings upon him and utmost greetings! Increase your praise. Praise is an angel with two eyes and two wings that flies to God directly to ask forgiveness for its reciter until Judgment Day."

Then the Prophet continued his way, riding on the Buraq together with all the angels that came to greet and accompany him. Whenever he passed through a different universe he found the angels

of that universe gathered to greet and dress him with all kinds of gifts and adornments. They dressed him with the cloaks of perfection and made him the possessor of every beauty.

Then the Prophet heard a very powerful voice coming from the Archangel Israfil from behind the veils of Lordly Power and Angelic Perfection:

> "O Paradises and heavens! O angels! O mountains and trees and oceans and rivers! O moons and suns and stars and planets and constellations! Plunge in to the beauty and perfection of the Prophet. O angels and houris of Paradise, walk with pride! O creation, be happy tonight, for we are receiving in our presence the Master of human beings and the Seal of Prophets."

Another voice came from an angel called Ishmael, saying:

> "O heavenly stairs, show yourselves and descend!" upon which the ladder of heaven descended all the way from Firdaws, the loftiest Paradise, until it reached the Temple of Solomon. The arms of the ladder shone with two heavenly lights, red amethyst and green jasper of the greatest perfection. Every believer is going to see that ladder and climb on it. It has one hundred steps and it goes from the Temple to the First Heaven.

Gabriel called the Prophet and the Buraq climbed the first step. There the Prophet saw all kinds of angels, red in color. On the second step, the Prophet saw angels in yellow cloth, on the third step the angels were green and all of them were greeting him and giving him heavenly gifts which he took and gave to Gabriel to keep as a trust for the believers on earth. On the fourth step messenger-angels came and said: "O Gabriel, keep rising for the Lord is waiting!" And the Prophet saw their subtle bodies shining and their faces glittering like mirrors in the sun.

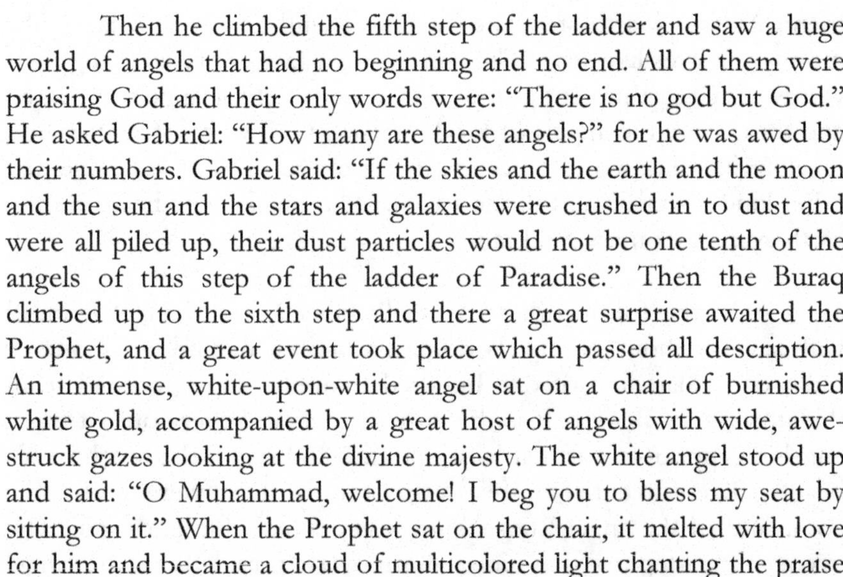

Then he climbed the fifth step of the ladder and saw a huge world of angels that had no beginning and no end. All of them were praising God and their only words were: "There is no god but God." He asked Gabriel: "How many are these angels?" for he was awed by their numbers. Gabriel said: "If the skies and the earth and the moon and the sun and the stars and galaxies were crushed in to dust and were all piled up, their dust particles would not be one tenth of the angels of this step of the ladder of Paradise." Then the Buraq climbed up to the sixth step and there a great surprise awaited the Prophet, and a great event took place which passed all description. An immense, white-upon-white angel sat on a chair of burnished white gold, accompanied by a great host of angels with wide, awe-struck gazes looking at the divine majesty. The white angel stood up and said: "O Muhammad, welcome! I beg you to bless my seat by sitting on it." When the Prophet sat on the chair, it melted with love for him and became a cloud of multicolored light chanting the praise of God. Out of every drop of that cloud God created another throne and another great angel sitting upon that throne.

Then the Buraq climbed to the seventh heaven and the Prophet saw angels whose light replaced the light of his vision, as in the case when someone looks at the sun and his sight is stolen away. At that time, he became able to see whatever these angels were seeing. Then he climbed the eighth step of the ladder and saw nothing but angels in prostration. He quickly climbed to the ninth so as not to disturb them. On the ninth step of the ladder he saw angels which passed description and he stood in awe, unable to comprehend their creation. At that time their leader appeared and said: "O Prophet! We are dressing you with the secret of our creation and enabling you to understand all things by God's permission."

Then the Prophet went up to the tenth step of the ladder and saw the angels that praised God in all the languages that had been created since the beginning of creation. The Prophet wondered at the limitless creations of God. At the eleventh step, the angels numbered even more than the angels of the fifth step, and out of them an infinite number of colors glowed, different for each single one of

them. At the twelfth step, the Prophet found angels with faces like moons and eyes like stars. The light of their faces were covering their words. On the thirteenth step, the most beautiful angels appeared and these were the angels of God, praising God with soft voices and reveling in other-worldly beauty. Their music did not resemble any other kind of music and if one tone of that music were heard on the earth everyone on it would faint.

On the fourteenth step the Prophet saw the angel Ishmael with seventy thousand angels riding on horses. Behind every one of them was a battalion of one hundred thousand angels created from the attribute of Beauty. It is the duty of each and every one of these angels to appear on earth at least one time to bring it the touch of his beauty. The fifteenth to the twenty-fourth steps were under the command of the angel Ruqya'il, great and small, thin and wide. The twenty-fifth step to the ninety-ninth were presided by the angel Qala'il. His right hand was under the first heaven. Between each two of his fingers there are seven hundred thousand angels continuously praising God. For each of the praises that they utter strings of pearls come out of their mouth. The diameter of every pearl is eighty-one miles. For each pearl God creates an angel that guards it and keeps it as a trust for human beings until they enter Paradise.

Then the Prophet saw a huge throne from a precious element other than gold standing on five posts. Each post has two wings and each wing encompasses the constellation of our world five times. On each wing rest fifty thousand angels, each of whom ask forgiveness for human beings in a different dialect and yet in complete harmony and with an angelic sound that melts the rocks of the seven earths. Out of each one of their tears God creates fifty thousand angels more whose task is to ask forgiveness in the same way as these angels do and in many times more dialects than they. Then the throne spoke to the Prophet and said: "I and the angels who guard me were created to carry human beings to their stations in Paradise." Then, the throne invited the Prophet to sit on it, and when he sat he felt a pleasure he had never experienced before.

## The First Paradise: The Abode of Peace

The Prophet arrived at the hundredth step where he heard the angels praising and glorifying their Lord in the First Heaven. It is called Dar al-Salam, the Abode of Peace, and has one hundred and twenty-four thousand doors. Each door represents a prophet. Gabriel knocked at the door reserved for the Prophet Muhammad. A voice said from inside: "Who it it?" Gabriel replied: "It is Gabriel and the Prophet Muhammad." The voice said: "Has he been sent for?" Gabriel said: "Yes, he has been called to the Divine Presence." The door was opened. The angel Ishmael came on a horse of light, covered in a cloth of light, holding a staff of light. In his right hand, Ishmael carried all the deeds of human beings performed during the day, and in the other, all that they had done during the night. One thousand processions of angels accompanied him.

Ishmael said: "O Gabriel, who is with you?" He replied: "The Prophet Muhammad, Peace be upon him." Ishmael said: "Has he been sent for?" Gabriel replied yes. Then the Buraq was invited to land on the first Paradise, the nearest Paradise to the world. It is also called al-*sama al-dunya*: the nearest Heaven. This Paradise can be compared to a rolling wave held in mid-air; God spoke to it and said: "Be a red emerald," and it was. The praising of its inhabitants is: *Subhana dhil Mulki wal Malakut*: "Praise be to the Possessor of the Earthly and the Heavenly Dominions."

Then the Prophet looked at the First Heaven and found an angel formed like a man. Al the actions that belong to human beings are displayed to him. If the spirit of a believer comes to him he sends it to Paradise; if the spirit of an unbeliever comes to him he asks

forgiveness for it. When forgiveness is granted he sends it to Paradise. He has a tablet made of light which hangs from the Throne to the first heaven. He writes on it the names of those who are sent to Paradise. Then the Prophet saw a man with an angelic power towards whom he felt a great attraction. When he asked who that man was, Gabriel said: "This is your father, Adam." Adam greeted him and said to the Prophet: "Welcome to the good son and the righteous Prophet."

There are two doors to the right and the left of Adam. When he looks at the right side he is happy and when he looks at the left he weeps. The Prophet asked what these two doors were. Gabriel said: "The door to the right is the door to Paradise and Rewards. When Adam sees his children entering it he smiles and is happy. The door to the left leads to punishment and the fire. When Adam sees his children entering it he weeps and is sad for them. Out of each of his tears God creates an angel who asks forgiveness until the day when forgiveness is granted and they are allowed to enter into Paradise."

Then the angels began to recite poetry:

*I yearn to see the one whom God created*
*to be unique in creation!*
*No beloved one is purer or more elevated than that one;*
*God's beloved is His servant, the Praised One*
*Whose name was cut out from the name*
*Of the Most Glorious One.*
*His are the attributes that no eloquence can express.*
*It is enough honor that for him the moon split in two.*
*What more do you ask than God's perfecting of his beauty?*
*And verily God endowed him with the best character.*
*And verily God created his light to be the greatest blessing,*
*And He called him "beloved" before He created creation.*
*And because of his light the sun was clouded over,*
*Because of his overwhelming light filling the firmament.*
*The clouds showed a great miracle and moved*
*Like a wild herd,*

*And thunder clapped and rain poured*
*Upon his mere request.*
*What more do you want than the softening of the rock*
*When he walked upon it with his sandaled feet,*
*Although you did not see its marks*
*When he tread on the sand?*
*God has elevated him to His presence*
*And the angelic world.*
*Were it not for him, there would never be Paradise,*
*Nor heavens, and no earth.*
*What an honor God bestowed upon him when He gave*
*Ten salutations to those who would*
*Send to him only one!"*

They moved for five hundred thousand light-years within the radius of the First Paradise. The Buraq moved faster than the speed of light, for each of its steps could reach wherever his sight did. The entire distances they traveled were filled with angels whose number is known only to the Creator, praising Him and glorifying Him with all kinds of praises. There was not one handful of space but it was occupied by an angel in prostration. They were all sizes, big and small. A voice came saying: "O My beloved Muhammad! All these angels are glorifying Me, and I am sending all this praise as waves upon waves of angelic blessings to support human beings through their daily life. These blessings will guide them towards everything that concerns them, and open for them all kinds of physical and spiritual knowledges that will help them progress in their ways of life, materially and spiritually. I will raise them through this angelic power and enable them to enter My Paradises when they come to My Divine Presence."

## The Second Paradise: the Abode of Constancy

Then Gabriel ordered the Buraq to take the Prophet to the second Paradise, whose name is *Dar al-Qarar*, the Abode of Constancy. He then knocked at one of the doors of the Second Paradise. It was made of a heavenly element that has no name in our language. The angel Jarja'il came with one thousand processions of angels who made an even greater and happier music than the angels of the First Paradise. A voice said:

"Who is it?"

"Gabriel."

"Who is accompanying you?"

"Muhammad, the Prophet of Mercy."

Then the door was opened. The Prophet saw angels whose faces were like the disk of the sun, riding horses and girded with spiritual swords and lances. The Prophet asked: "O Gabriel! Who are these?" Gabriel answered: "These are angels whom God created to support human against devils. Their praising is: *Subhana dhil 'Izzati wal Jabarut*: 'Glory to the Lord of Force and Might,' and they are wearing yellow turbans on their heads. When they praise God their turbans move and radiate a yellow light that supports the light of the sun. They radiate another light also, which makes the devils run away and chases out gossip from the heart of believers." Then the Prophet saw two very handsome men sitting on a throne made of red rubies. He asked: "Who are these?" Gabriel said: "They are your relatives, John and Jesus." Jesus was of a reddish complexion as if he came out of the bath. Then angels came to the Prophet in battalions, greeting him one by one. God extended time in such a way that one second was enough to greet all of the angels and pray with them, for the time of prayer had come. Jesus and John greeted the Prophet farewell, and Gabriel ordered the Buraq to go to the Third Paradise.

## The Third Paradise: The Abode of Eternity

The Prophet moved in space for another five hundred thousand light-years until they reached the third Paradise. It is called Dar al-khuld: the Abode of Eternity. As they approached their destination they heard great voices that thundered all around them. "That is the sound of angels praising their Lord," said Gabriel. As they approached they heard the music of the angels by which everything moves in the orbits of the heavenly worlds. Gabriel stopped at a door made of a pure, burnished heavenly copper, and he knocked. "Who is there?" said a voice behind the door.

"Gabriel, bringing Muhammad."

"Has he been sent for?"

"Yes." And the door was opened.

The Prophet entered and he saw an angel who changed from one shape to another in every moment. As he changed, his color changed also. He seemed as one moving in a flash and yet immobile like a moving series of pictures and yet each picture is fixed in its place. Behind the angel the Prophet saw seven hundred thousand angels, all of them moving like the first angel, from one colorful image into another, like countless kaleidoscopes. Their feet reached the seven earths. Their musical praise was: *Subhana al-hayy al-qayyum alladhi la yamut*: "Glory to the Living One, the Self-Subsistent who never dies!" The melody of their praise moved the entire heavens to unutterable joy which showered mercy on the earth and its inhabitants. The Prophet asked Gabriel to ask the angel whether human beings could hear that music and if it were possible for them. The angel said: "Anyone who opens his angelic power and connects

himself to us will hear that melody and he will receive the reward that we receive for uttering this praise." Then the angel recited:

*Secret Reality! Angelic heart of light,*
*Kingdom of power, shining in steadfast light,*
*Firm in foundation, in beauty all complete,*
*Its essence descended from Adam's heart enthroned,*
*Just as the All-Merciful descended on His Throne.*
*Essence of angels' light in Adam manifest,*
*And yoked with it Gods' trust fulfilled,*
*The grant He made to all mankind.*
*Here appeared knowledge of God's light*
*Known only to chosen saints who alone can see.*
*Where His knowledge glows imperfection flees*
*And all worldly cares dim and disappear.*
*Here ends and begins the place of drawing near*
*Where the pure ones settled, similar to light upon light.*

As they moved forward they saw a handsome man before whose beauty everything paled. "This is Joseph, the Prophet," said Gabriel. The Prophet Muhammad approached him and greeted him, and Joseph greeted him back with the best greeting of heaven. Gabriel said: "Out of the beauty of Joseph came the beauty of all human beings. His is the beauty of the full moon, the sun and the stars." Yearning for angelic beauty will melt the hearts of the stone-hearted. The faint-hearted cannot hope to approach its secret, for they will immediately fall under its power and extinguish themselves in it. That is the meaning of the sweetness of painful yearning in love: the approach of beauty in its absence is sweeter still than its embrace and possession. For possession of the beloved entails the satisfaction of the lower self, while to remain in pain because of the beloved is better than comfort and contentment.

Behind Joseph the Prophet saw a great human crowd, all of them wearing radiant angelic dresses. The Prophet asked, "Who are these people, O Gabriel?" He answered: "Behind Joseph God created seven hundred thousand posts in Paradise; on each post there are seven hundred thousand red jewels; each jewel contains seven hundred thousand palaces; in every palace there are seven hundred thousand rooms, and in every room there are seven hundred thousand windows. These rooms are inhabited by human beings who carry angelic powers and spend their lives in love of each other and nature. Their hearts are filled with love of Me and devoid of low desires. They pine for Me and I pine for them. Every day these human beings appear at their windows and look at the people of Paradise. From their beauty a great light shines forth, in the same way that the sun appears in the windows of the sky and sheds its light over the people on earth. Then the people of Paradise say: 'Let us run towards the Lovers of God.' As soon as they reach them these Lovers adorn them with all kinds of rainbows and showers of light. They give them a dress made of green silk which symbolizes the qualities of those made perfect and agreeable to God."

## The Fourth Paradise: the Sheltering Garden

Then Gabriel called for prayer and the Prophet led the prayer among all the inhabitants of Paradise. Then the Buraq moved for another five hundred thousand light-years during which they traveled towards the fourth heaven which is called Jannat al-Ma'wa: the Sheltering Garden. There they heard a voice mixing angels and spirits. The door of the Prophet was made of silver upon a floor of gold. Again, the voice behind the door asked: "Who is there?" and Gabriel answered, "Muhammad."

"Has he been sent for?"

"Yes." And the door opened.

The Prophet saw angels standing and sitting, lying and bowing, praising and saying: "*Subhan al-malik al-quddus rabb al-mala'ikati war ruh,*" : "Glory to the holiest King, Lord of the angels and the Spirit!" The Prophet asked Gabriel, "O Gabriel, is that not the prayer of my grandfather Abraham?" and Gabriel said, "Yes, this is how your grandfather Abraham used to pray, and God was so happy with that prayer that he created an entire host of angels and filled the fourth heaven with them. He ordered them to repeat the same prayer. If anyone recites that praising among human beings, God will give them rewards according to the number of these angels."

Then the Prophet saw two angels, one of transparent crystal like spring water, and one denser like salt water. Gabriel said: "One is the angel of sweet waters. He carries all the oceans of this universe with his right thumb. The other is the angel of salty waters. He carries all the oceans of this universe in his left thumb. These are the angels responsible for supporting every creature in creation through water, sweet or salty. They meet without mixing, as God has said:

> *He hath loosed the two seas. They meet. There is a barrier between them. They encroach not one upon the other.*[49]

Behind them the Prophet saw angels shaped like birds, standing on the bank of a great river of Paradise. When a human being on earth says: "There is no god but God," one of these angel-birds opens his wings. If the person says: "Glory to God," the angel-bird enters the river to swim in it. When the person says: "Praise be to God," the angel-bird dives into the water. When the person says: "God is greatest," the angel-bird comes out of the river. When the person says: "There is neither power nor might except in God," the angel-bird will shake off the water from him, and seventy thousand drops of water will come from him, out of each of which God

---

[49] Surat ar-Rahman, 55:19-20

creates an angel that asks forgiveness for that person until Judgment Day. In addition to this, God orders forty thousand rewards written in the book of that one and keeps them for him until his resurrection.

Then the Prophet saw a man who leaned against the Books of human beings, in which were inscribed all their deeds. The Prophet asked: "Who is this?" Gabriel said: "This is the Prophet Idris, Peace be upon him." The Prophet approached Idris and greeted him. Idris greeted him back and said: "Welcome to the pious brother and perfect prophet." Above him the Prophet saw a dome of light on which was written: "There is no god but God, and Muhammad is His Messenger." The Prophet looked inside it and saw a venerable old man with a white beard filled with light and crowned with a white turban. He asked: "Who is that, O Gabriel?" He answered: "That is an angel representing the Prophet Idris." The Prophet greeted him and said: "O my brother! God has elevated you and honored you, and you have entered Paradise before me and saw its pleasures." Idris said: "O Beloved one! At first I did not enter Paradise nor see its pleasure. But when I left this world I entered a garden on which door I saw: 'Beyond this door none may enter before Muhammad and his nation.' And I asked God, 'For the sake of my grandson Muhammad, let me in.' God let me in, so now because of you I am in this place."

Then Idris recited:

*"This Station sought by all for shelter,*
*This lofty place where all people bow subdued*
*And stands the noble Messenger*
*With wisdom and might endued,*
*Station of guidance and angelic light*
*Where gloom of night and orphans' sadness*
*At once are effaced,*
*This is the Station of direct communication*
*And the firm foothold for those determined to reach.*
*The All-Merciful called him His beloved one*

*And he is the beloved one of the universe*
*And from his light came the light of all life."*

## The Fifth Paradise: The Garden of Beauty and Felicity

The Prophet traveled for five hundred thousand light-years, after which he arrived at the fifth Paradise which is called Jannat al-Naʿim: "the Garden of Beauty and Felicity." Its door is made of mixed gold and silver from heaven. Gabriel knocked at the door and a voice said: "Who is it?"

"Gabriel, bringing the Prophet, Peace be upon him."

"Has he been sent for?"

"Yes."

"Welcome, O Beloved one, to the fifth Paradise!"

The door opened and the Prophet saw five beautiful ladies whose radiant light among their servants made them appear like diamonds surrounded by pearls. His heart was moved towards them. He asked Gabriel: "Who are these ladies?"

He answered: "This is Eve, the mother of human beings, this is the Virgin Mary, the mother of Jesus, this is Moses' mother Yukabid, and this is Assia, the wife of Pharaoh."

The fifth lady looked like a sun among stars. Her light shone over the rest of the inhabitants of that Paradise like a gentle breeze passing through the tree-leaves.

Gabriel said: "This is an angel representing your daughter Fatima, O Prophet!"

The Prophet asked: "Gabriel, what is the secret of this Paradise?"

Gabriel said: "God created this Paradise to reflect the beauty and perfection of women. The light of this Paradise is the source of the angelic lights of all women on earth. Women have been created to carry the secret of creation in themselves. God has honored them greatly by making their wombs the repository of His word which represents the Spirit. He looks at the most sacred place and there descends His mercy and blessings. He perfected that place and covered it with three protective layers to shelter it from any damage. The first is a layer of light, the second a layer of love, and the third a layer of beauty. There he fashions and creates human beings after His likeness, as the Prophet said: 'God created Adam after His likeness' He orders the angels of the womb to perfect His creation by giving the baby life, beauty, health, intelligence, and all kinds of perfect attributes that will make each one distinguished among human beings."

"Women are not created weaker but more generous than men. They are created more beautiful and less fierce, as beauty hates to hurt and harm others. That is why they seem weak to people, but in reality they are not. Angels are the strongest of created beings, and women are closer to the angelic nature than men, as they are readier than men to carry angelic light. It is the good manners and ethics of spirituality which they carry which makes them less forceful than men. Even physically, however, they are extremely strong. They undergo great upheavals in their body without flinching for the sake of childbirth, and face the direst physical conditions more

successfully than men because God has enabled them to insure the survival of generations."

"God gave women five angelic qualities which men rarely have. They are the source of peace, as God said that He created them "*so that ye might find rest in them.*"[50] This is the attribute of the first Paradise which is named "the Abode of Peace."

- They are oases of constancy in the midst of chaos and change. That is why they give birth as the mother nurtures and shelters the baby more reliably than the father. This is the attribute of the Second Paradise, which is named 'the Abode of Constancy.'

- They perpetuate generations. Through their offspring God creates angelic prophets and saints who establish His perpetual remembrance on earth as the angels establish it in Heaven. This is the attribute of the Third Paradise which is named 'the Abode of Eternity.'

- They are generous and bountiful. They are described as 'a fertile land' in all Scriptures because they give without counting, including life.

- They sacrifice themselves for the sake of another creation, and this is the attribute of the Fourth Paradise which is named 'the Sheltering Garden.'

- Finally, they are the source of Beauty. Through their softness and subtlety, God has crowned the earth with the diadem of angelic grace. This is the attribute of the Fifth Paradise which is named "the Garden of Beauty."

---

[50] Surah Rum: (Rome) 30:21.

## The Sixth Paradise: The Garden of Eden

The Prophet traveled again on the Buraq for five hundred thousand years. On his way to the Sixth Paradise which is called *Jannat Adn*: "the Garden of Eden," he saw nations and nations of saffron-colored angels standing on pedestals of pink marble. They had one thousand wings and on each wing there were one thousand faces. Each face had one thousand mouths saying: "Praise be to the Lord of Majesty and Splendor!" Gabriel knocked at the door of the Sixth Paradise which was made of aquamarine and gold. As usual, a voice asked from behind the door who was there and the answer was given: "Gabriel, bringing the Prophet, Peace be upon him." "Has he been sent for?" said the voice. "Yes," replied Gabriel. The door was opened. The Prophet entered and what he saw passed all imagination and all recorded books, all fabled accounts, all legends, all histories.

The Prophet traveled again on the Buraq for five hundred thousand years. On his way to the Sixth Paradise which is called *Jannat Adn*: "the Garden of Eden," he saw nations and nations of saffron-colored angels standing on pedestals of pink marble. They had one thousand wings and on each wing there were one thousand faces. Each face had one thousand mouths saying: "Praise be to the Lord of Majesty and Splendor!" Gabriel knocked at the door of the Sixth Paradise which was made of aquamarine and gold. As usual, a voice asked from behind the door who was there and the answer was given: "Gabriel, bringing the Prophet, Peace be upon him." "Has he been sent for?" said the voice. "Yes," replied Gabriel. The door was opened. The Prophet entered and what he saw passed all imagination and all recorded books, all fabled accounts, all legends, all histories.

*"O Prophet sprung from Hashim's line,*
*Lover of Him Who is lauded above,*
*Sealer of every book revealed to mankind.*
*Opener of treasured knowledge sublime*
*Who mounted the Buraq to ascend to his Lord,*
*The God in Whose presence none before had remained,*
*Approach that place where only angels draw near*
*O Messenger of God before whom winds and clouds move*
*And lay open clear myriad paths to celestial light.*
*For your intercession human souls plead and yearn,*
*O Prophet at whose sight angels delight!*
*It is you for whom Paradise was made and adorned,*
*For you the lote-tree of farthest limit is made to stand*
*And bear the fruit of compassion in every land.*
*O beloved Muhammad, may God grant us to be*
*Always numbered in your noble band."*

## The Seventh Paradise: *Jannat al-Firdaws*

The Prophet arrived at the Seventh Paradise whose roof touches the Heavenly Throne and whose name is *Jannat al-Firdaws*, after a travel of five hundred thousand light-years. He knocked at the door which was made of pure emerald, topaz, beryl, and gold. After he entered he saw another gate of light. From it came the praise of nations of hidden angels at whose sight one would die of awe because of their intense beauty. Their laud was simply: "Praise be to the Creator of Light!" Beyond this it is not permitted to speak about them. The Prophet greeted them with the greeting of peace and proceeded past the gate of gold to a dome of light which encompassed all the previous heavens, although the distance he had traveled between the sixth and the seventh heaven was the same as that between each two of the other layers of Paradise.

Inside the dome the Prophet saw an angelic being which resembled him in every fashion and who was leaning against a wall of white silk which seemed to move like a waterfall and yet stand firm. The Prophet asked who that was and Gabriel said: "This is your grandfather Abraham, the leader of the pure of heart and a great one among prophets." Abraham said: "Welcome to the pious son and the perfected Prophet!"

Around Abraham stood crowned angels. Each of their crowns contained four hundred diamonds, each worth more than what the entire earth contains. At their service stood throngs of angels crowned with the light of the previous angels and all were reading the Verse of the Throne. Gabriel said: "This is the verse that keeps the universe firm in the balance. This is the secret of the order of Creation." And the angels recited:

*God! There is no God save Him,*
*the Alive, the Eternal,*
*Neither slumber nor sleep overtaketh him.*
*Unto him belongeth whatsoever is in the heavens*
*and whatsoever is in earth.*
*Who is he that intercedeth with him save by His leave?*
*He knoweth that which is in front of them*
*And that which is behind them,*
*While they encompass nothing of His knowledge*
*Save what He will.*
*His Throne includeth the heavens and the earth,*
*And He is never weary of preserving them.*
*He is the Sublime, the Tremendous.* [51]

[51] Surat al-Baqara, 2:255

Circumambulating the building against which Abraham leaned, the entire universes, the throngs of angels of the seven heavens, the angels of mercy and the angels of wrath, the angels of beauty, the angels brought near, the great and the small angels, the visible and the invisible angels, and all the human beings whose angelic souls had been purified and elevated to the divine presence, the prophets, the truthful saints, the martyrs, the righteous, all of creation whirled and turned in the same direction as every heavenly body, counterclockwise, around the Kaaba of the heavens. The Prophet said: "O Gabriel, How wondrous are the incredible marvels of my Lord!" And Gabriel replied: "O Muhammad! you have seen only a glimpse of the wonders of God."

## The Lote-Tree of the Furthest Boundary

The Prophet and Gabriel traveled once more until they reached the absolute limit of the created intellect, named *Sidrat al-muntaha*: "The Lote-Tree of the Furthest Boundary." There they saw nothing which the tongue could describe. The effect of the sight they beheld on the Prophet is a secret which took place in his heart. A sound came to them from above which dissipated some of the Prophet's astonishment. At that time he saw a large tree which does not resemble any of the trees of Paradise, a tree without description, covering all the Paradises, heavens, and universes. The trunk of the Tree was a huge angel named Samrafil. The Prophet could see nothing else besides it. It grew from an infinite, unimaginable, indescribable ocean of musk. The tree had an infinite number of branches, created from a heavenly element that has no name in a created language. The distance between one branch and another was five hundred thousand light-years. On every branch there was an infinite number of leaves. If all the created universes were placed on a single one of these leaves they would disappear, like an atom disappears inside an ocean of water. On every leaf sat a huge angel in a multi-colored light. On his head was a crown of light and in his hand a staff of light. Written on their forehead was the inscription: "We are the inhabitants of the Lote-Tree." Their praise was: "Praise be to God Who has no end." Their names are the *Sarufiyyun* or Seraphim, "The Secret Ones," because they are created from the absolute secret of their Lord.

From the trunk of the tree four absolute springs issued. The first was a pure, transparent, crystal water; the second was a river of white milk; the third was a river of pleasurable, untarnished wine that elevates without abasing; the fourth was a river of pure honey mixed with gold. Inside the trunk was the prayer-niche of Gabriel, and his constant words of praise are:

*Allahu Akbar: God is Great!*

to which the reply always comes from above:

*Ana Akbar: I am Greater!*
*Ana Akbar: I am Greater!*

Gabriel entered his prayer-niche and he called for the prayer. All the Seraphim stood in rows and the Prophet led them in prayer. The prayer finished and all the Seraphim were ordered to give their greetings to the Prophet one after the other. After this, a great angel came out from behind Gabriel's prayer-niche and asked the Prophet to approach.

The Prophet and Gabriel entered the trunk of the tree and reached in a glance the entire sight of creation. On the top of the tree they saw Adam and Eve and Noah, Abraham, Moses, Jesus, and all the other prophets whom they had just visited. With them they saw all their respective nations, sitting with them in spirit together with those of the Prophet's nation who had already left this world. All

were sitting there together, happy, basking in the love and beauty of their Lord's mercy and praising Him.

That Lote-Tree carries the knowledge of all of God's creation from the beginning of its sequence in time. Whatever is created is part of it and contained in it. It was called the tree "of the furthermost boundary" because everything ends in it and after it begins a new life. God decorated it with the light of His own essence. It has three characteristics: a continuous shade of light extending over every creation, a continuous pleasure reaching everyone from the fruit of its branches, and a continuous fragrance from its flowers scenting with beauty the life of creation.

Then the Prophet and Gabriel moved forward. A stern and severe angel appeared and covered the horizon before them. Gabriel said: "O Prophet! this is the angel of death ʿAzra'il." The angel of death said: "Welcome, O Muhammad! you who bear goodness, and welcome to all the Prophets and their nations. This is the place from which I gaze at the destinies of every person and seize the spirits of those whom I am commanded to bring to eternal life."

The Prophet asked: "Tell me how you take the souls of the dying." The angel of death revealed to the Prophet: "When God orders me to take the spirit of a human being at the last hour of his life and the first hour of his afterlife, I send to him my deputies who carry with them the smell of Paradise and a branch from the tree of paradise which they put between his eyes. When that sweet smell reaches him and he catches a glimpse of that heavenly branch, his spirit is attracted and his soul begins to ascend to paradise, until it reaches his throat. At that time, I descend from my place and I take his spirit with the greatest care, because God wants this moment to be easy on His servant. I then carry his soul to Paradise. On the way, whenever I pass by angels, then angels will greet this soul and salute it until it reaches the presence of its Lord. God the Exalted says to that soul at that time: "Welcome to the good spirit which I created and placed in a good body! O my angels! write the upper layer of Paradise as a reward for that person." Then angels take him up to Paradise,

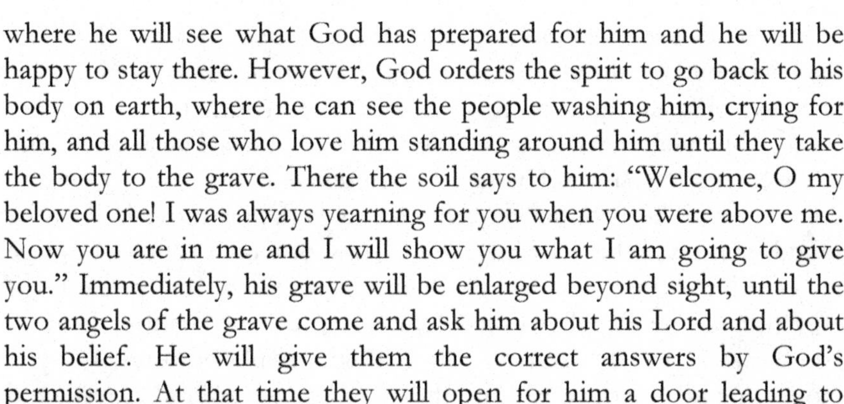

where he will see what God has prepared for him and he will be happy to stay there. However, God orders the spirit to go back to his body on earth, where he can see the people washing him, crying for him, and all those who love him standing around him until they take the body to the grave. There the soil says to him: "Welcome, O my beloved one! I was always yearning for you when you were above me. Now you are in me and I will show you what I am going to give you." Immediately, his grave will be enlarged beyond sight, until the two angels of the grave come and ask him about his Lord and about his belief. He will give them the correct answers by God's permission. At that time they will open for him a door leading to Paradise and his spirit will go back upward to the same place where God first called him to His presence."

*I remember when death had separated us.*

*I consoled myself with the thought of the Beloved Prophet.*
*I said: "All of us go on this way one day.*
*Who does not die today, he will die tomorrow.*
*Be happy, O my soul, because your Lord is waiting for you*
*And the beloved one is calling you."*

Then Gabriel moved forward another five hundred thousand light-years, mounted on the Buraq, until they reached a place where Gabriel began to slow down. The Prophet said: "O Gabriel! why are you slowing down? Are you leaving me?" Gabriel replied: "I cannot go further." The Prophet said:

"Gabriel, don't leave me alone." "O Muhammad!" Gabriel said, "You now have to step down from the Buraq and move to a place which no one has entered before you." At that moment the Buraq stopped and was unable to move further. The Prophet stepped down and moved hesitantly. Gabriel said: "O Prophet, move forward without fear. If I were to continue with you I would be annihilated for the greatness of the Light."

The Prophet moved, and moved, and moved. He saw Michael standing ahead of him, afraid and trembling. The light of his face was changing quickly from one color to another. The Prophet asked: "Michael, is this your station?" "Yes," Michael answered, "and if I were to trespass it I would be annihilated. But you go on and don't stop." The Prophet moved, and moved, and moved. Then he found Israfil with his four huge wings, one of which covered his face to veil him from the light which came from the horizon of everything. The Prophet asked him: "Is this your station, Israfil?" Israfil said, "Yes. If I trespassed it that light would burn me. But you move on and do not fear." And the Prophet moved, and moved, and moved. He saw the Spirit to whom God gave the power of earth and the heavens. From the top of his head to the bottom of his feet and from every cell of his there were faces with traits of subtle light, the number of which no one knows but God, and from the each of which God creates an angel-spirit which looks like the Spirit, whom He then takes to himself as the spirit-angels of the Divine Presence.

Every day the Spirit looks into hell three times, and because of the cool light of his angelic gaze the fire of hell melts until it becomes as a rainbow. The Spirit also looks into Paradise three times every day and extends to it the divine light which God gives him. If God gathered the tears of the eyes of the Spirit it would flood all the created universes and make Noah's flood seem like the drop gathered by an needle dipped into the ocean. This is the Spirit whom God mentioned in the Quran:

"The day when the Spirit and the angels rise, no one shall speak except with permission from His Lord."

The Prophet said: "O Spirit! is this your station?" The spirit replied: "Yes, and if I trespass it I will be annihilated by the light which I am receiving. O Muhammad! Move forward and do not be afraid. You are invited and you have permission." The Prophet moved forward. God inspired his heart with the following discourse: "I the Lord, have veiled myself from the inhabitants of Paradise, as I have veiled myself from the inhabitants of the earth. As I veiled

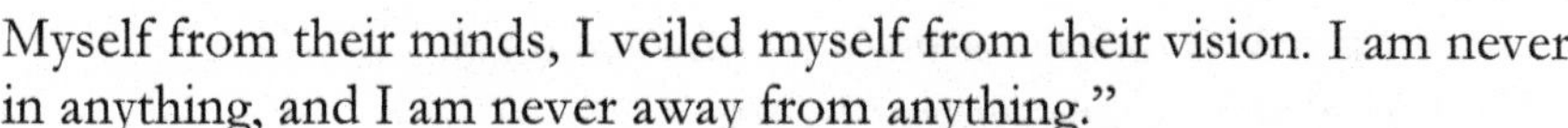


Myself from their minds, I veiled myself from their vision. I am never in anything, and I am never away from anything."

The Prophet then moved through one veil after another until he passed through one thousand veils. Finally he opened the Veil of Oneness. He found himself like a lamp suspended in the middle of a divine air. He saw a magnificent, great and unutterable matter. He asked his Lord to give him firmness and strength. He felt that a drop of that presence was put on his tongue and he found it cooler than ice and sweeter than honey. Nothing on earth and the seven paradises tasted like it. With this drop, God put into the Prophet's heart the knowledge of the First and the Last, the heavenly and the earthly. All this was revealed to him in one instant shorter than the fastest second. He was ordered to move forward. As he moved he found himself elevated on a throne that can never be described, now or later. Three additional drops were given to him: one on his shoulder consisting in majesty, one in his heart consisting in mercy, and an additional one on his tongue which consisted in eloquence. Then a voice came from that presence, which no created being had heard before: "O Muhammad! I have made you the intercessor for everyone." At that moment the Prophet felt his mind enraptured and taken away to be replaced with an astonishing secret. He was placed in the Fields of God's Eternity and Endlessness. In the first he found no beginning and in the second he found no end. Then God revealed to Him: "My end is in My beginning and My beginning is in My end." Then the Prophet knew that all doors were absolutely closed except those that led to God, that God cannot be described within the confine of a place in speech, and that God encompasses the everywhere of all places. This is a secret that no tongue can be stirred to express, no door opened to reveal, and no answer can define. He is the Guide to Himself and the Lord of His own description. He is the Beauty of all beauty and the speech by which to describe Himself belongs to Him alone.

*O God My Creator, in Your infinity do I stand amazed.*
*In Your ocean of unity do I drown submerged.*
*O God, at times You closet me in familiar intimacy.*

*At times You leave me without, veiled and strange,*
*Hidden in Your sovereign Majesty.*
*Give me to drink the wine of Your love,*
*For only drunk from it am I able to say:*
*My Lord! Let me see You.*

The Prophet then looked on his right and saw nothing except His Lord, then on his left and saw nothing except his Lord, then to the front, to the back, and above him, and he saw nothing except his Lord. He hated to leave that honored and blessed place. But God said: "O Muhammad, you are a messenger to My servants as all messengers, if you stay here you would never be able to communicate My Message. Therefore descend back to earth, and communicate My message to My servants. Whenever you want to be in the same state as you are now, make your prayers, and I shall open this state for you." This is why the Prophet stated: "Prayer is the apple of my eyes," and he called it also: "Our rest."

Then the Prophet was ordered to go back to earth, but he left the self in heaven and his spirit at the Lote-tree, and his heart in the unutterable divine presence while his secret was left suspended without place. His self wondered: "Where is the heart?" and the Heart wondered: "Where is the spirit?" and the spirit wondered: "Where is the secret?" and the secret wondered where it was. And God revealed: "O self of the Prophet! I granted you the blessing and the forgiveness, and O spirit! I granted you the mercy and the honor, and O heart! I granted you the Love and the Beauty, and O secret, you have Me." God then revealed to the Prophet the order to recite:

*He is the one who sends blessings on you, together with His angels, in order to bring you out from darkness into light.*[52]

"O Muhammad! I have ordered the angels of all My heavens, those created and those yet uncreated, to send blessings on you and My creation unceasingly, with My own praise. I am your Lord Who said: My Mercy has overtaken My anger. And all My angels I have

52 Surat al-Ahzab, 33:43

created for you human beings." And God ordered the Prophet to descend with this angelic message back to earth.

# PART TWO
# -THE PRESENT

A
Journey
to the Land
of Angels

A certain saint is sitting day and night in his room praising and meditating. One day he heard sounds outside his room and footsteps approaching. The sound of the footsteps increases until he imagines there is a huge crowd waiting for him outside his room. He opens the door and sees a crowd of five thousand angels huddled at his door, gathered in a blinding white light recalling the verse:

> *Praise be to God, the Creator of the heavens and the earth, who appointeth the angels messengers having wings two, three and four. He multiplieth in creation what He will. Lo! God is Able to do all things.*[53] .

The saint says to them: "Who are you?" "We are the angels of the Lord," replies one of them. "We were sent to ask you if you needed anything because:

> *He it is who blesseth you, and His angels bless you, that He may bring you forth from darkness into light; and He is Merciful to the believers.*[54]

The saint responds, "I have but one request: I would like to meet my Lord." They say: "Whoever likes to meet his Lord, His Lord likes to meet him. Repeat after us." They mention some words that he does not understand but which he repeats nonetheless. He finds himself lifted out of his body. The saint sees every angel carrying a chrysanthemum from Paradise exuding a blissful scent. They accompany him to the first heaven, where he is welcomed by guards who say: "Welcome to the pious saint of God! You have been invited because of your love to meet your Lord." He is surrounded by glittering lights that please his eyes and all kinds of white and green birds flying everywhere. The angels show him his place in Paradise. There he sees angels going up and down on heavenly stairs.

---

[53] Surat Fatir, 35:1

[54] Surat al-Ahzab, 33:43

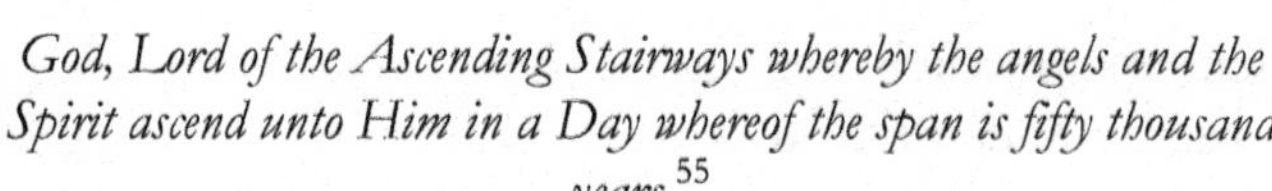

*God, Lord of the Ascending Stairways whereby the angels and the Spirit ascend unto Him in a Day whereof the span is fifty thousand years.*[55]

They seat him on a throne of gold ornamented with heavenly pearls and jewels. Then he sees the angels of the first heaven standing in a circle, those of the second heaven sitting behind them, those of the third, fourth, fifth, sixth, and seventh heavens standing and sitting in successive circles, praising and singing to their Lord. Then a great light blazes forth and he immediately faints. That light was coming from the Divine Presence. He finds himself back in his body as he had left it. As he wakes up he hears the voice of an angel whispering in his ears: "That is the reward of every righteous person in this world."

One of the greatest saints, Abdullah al-Daghestani, fought in the Dardanelles in his twenties. He brought back the following account:

> One day there was an attack from the enemy and about a hundred of us were left behind to defend a frontier. I was an excellent marksman, able to hit a thread from a great distance. We were unable to defend our position and were under fierce attack. I felt a bullet strike my heart and I fell to the ground, mortally wounded.
>
> As I lay dying, I saw the Prophet coming to me. He said, "O my son, you were destined to die her, but we still need you on this earth in both your spiritual and physical form. I come to you to show you how a person dies and how the angel of death takes the soul." He presented me in a vision in which I saw my body, cell by cell, beginning from the toes. As life was withdrawing, I could see how many cells are in my body, the function of every cell, the cure for every

[55] Surat al-Maʿarij, 70:3-4

sickness of each cell and I hard every cell in its remembrance of God.

As my soul was passing away, I experienced what a person feels when he dies. I was brought to se the different states of death: painful states of death; easy states of death, and the most blissful states of death. I enjoyed that passing so much because I was going back to my origin which made me comprehend the secret of the Quranic verse:

*To God we belong and to Him is our return.*[56]

That vision continued until I experienced my soul departing on the last breath. I saw the angel of death come and heard the questions he would ask. I experienced the kinds of visions that appear to the dying, yet I was alive during that experience and this enabled me to understand the secret of that state.

I saw in a vision my soul looking down on my body. The Prophet told me, "come with me!" I accompanied the Prophet and he took me to a vision of the seven heavens. He raised me to the station of truthfulness where I met all the prophets, all the saints, all the martyrs, and all the righteous.

He said, "O my son! Now you are going to see the tortures of hell." There I saw everything that the Prophet had mentioned in the Traditions about the tortures and punishments of that place. I said, "O Prophet! You who were sent as a Mercy for human beings, is there not any way for these people to be saved?" He replied, "Yes, my son! They can be saved with my intercession. I am showing you what the fate

56 Surat al-Baqara, 2:156

of those people would be if I did not have the power to intercede for them. O my son! Now I will return you to earth and to your body."

As soon as the Prophet said this I looked down and saw my body looking somewhat swollen. I said, "O Prophet of God! It is better to be here with you. I do not want to go back. I am happy with you in the Divine Presence. Look at that world. I have already been there and now I have left. Why must I go back? Look, my body is swollen."

He said, "O my son, you must go back. That is your duty. By the order of the Prophet I went back to my body, even though I did not want to. I saw that the bullet in my heart had been encased in flesh and the bleeding had stopped. As I smoothly re-entered my body, the vision ended. When it did, I saw the medics on the field of battle looking for the survivors among the dead. One of them said, "That one is alive! That one is alive!"

They took me and treated me until I recovered and my health was restored. Then they sent me back to my uncle. As soon as I reached him, he told me, "O my son, did you enjoy your visit?" I did not say yes and I did not say no, as I wanted to know if he meant the visit to the army or the visit in the company of the Prophet. Then he asked me again, "O my son, did you enjoy your visit with the Prophet ?" I realized that he knew everything that had happened to me. I ran to him, kissed his hand, and told him, "O my shaykh! I went with the Prophet and I must admit that I did not want to come back, but he told me that it was my duty."

# The Spirit

God created one of His greatest beings and named him "The Spirit." (*al-ruh*).

> *He sendeth down the angels with the Spirit of His command unto whom He will of His bondsmen, saying: Warn mankind that there is no god save Me, so keep your duty unto Me!*[57]

He is also named Hajib Allah: "God's Gatekeeper." He is an angel-spirit. His mouth alone can contain all the angels God has created. He always stands before God. On the Day of Judgment, all human beings will see him and feel awe at his greatness and majesty:

> *On the day when the angels and the Spirit stand arrayed, they speak not, saving him whom the Beneficent alloweth and who speaketh right.*[58]

He has ten thousand wings. If he were to open only two of them, they would cover the entire firmament from East to West. When God orders him to fly and travel in this universe, he only needs to use two wings to travel at the speed of thought, which is unimaginably greater than the speed of light. He has seventy thousand eyes, seventy thousand ears, seventy thousand mouths, and seventy-thousand tongues. He is in the fourth heaven and he is greater than all the created universes. He is brought nearer to God than all the angels as he is the most honorable one among them. He is the custodian of revelation. He was created in the image of a human being. He praises God continuously, and for each one of his praises God creates one angel-spirit resembling him. In a day and a night he praises God more numerously than the number of stars in the created universes. Whenever God sends any angel on earth, He orders the Spirit to send one of the angel-spirits to accompany that angel.

---

[57] Surat al-Nahl, 16:2

[58] Surat an-Naba, 78:38

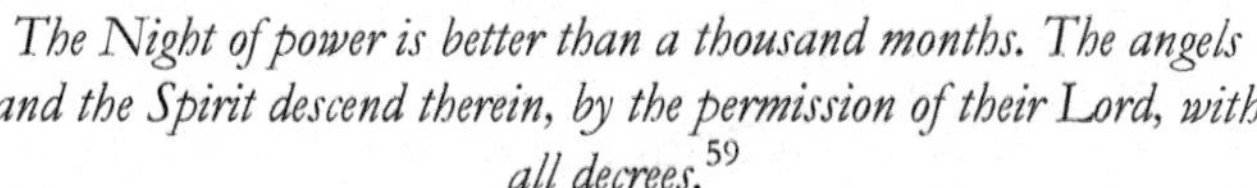

*The Night of power is better than a thousand months. The angels and the Spirit descend therein, by the permission of their Lord, with all decrees.*[59]

The Prophet Muhammad said: "Spirits are an angelic array different from angels, resembling human beings although they are not human beings. They have a head, hands, and legs." Human beings, angels, spiritual beings (jinn), and devils are one tenth of the number of angel-spirits. Angel-spirits eat and drink. In the hereafter there will be two groups of angelic beings standing before God: one group consists in angels, the other is angel-spirits. Human beings and jinns form ten parts: the former are one part out of ten, the latter nine. Jinn and angels also form ten parts: the former are one part out of ten, the latter nine. Similarly, angels and angel-spirits form ten parts: angels are one part out of ten, angel-spirits nine. Furthermore, the angel-spirits and the cherubim form ten parts: the former are one, the latter nine out of the ten.

Angel-spirits are the guardian angels of angels but cannot be seen except by a select few of them, just as the angels cannot be seen by human beings except by a select few.

*They will ask thee concerning the Spirit. Say: The Spirit is by command of my Lord, and of knowledge ye have been vouchsafed but little*[60]

The Archangel Gabriel has his own station beyond which he cannot go, lest he be annihilated. Before him there is Michael, also standing at his station, serious, afraid before God. Above him also is Israfil, the angel of the Trumpet-call. Above that station is the Spirit, who is above all angels while they cannot see him, because he veils himself from them with seventy thousand veils of reflected light and seventy thousand more veils of original light.

---

[59] Surat al-Qadr, 97:3-4

[60] Surat an-Najm, 17:85

# Angelic Miracles

The year is 1982, in Beirut, Lebanon, the jewel city of the Middle East which Westerners used to describe as "the Switzerland of the Middle East." It is the middle of the Lebanese crisis. Local tyrants are fighting each other and shelling the city with over three hundred rockets a minute raining on both sides, indifferent to the victims. On a very dark day of severe bombing, everyone in our ten-story building is huddled in their apartments praying. Each person hopes to escape with his or her own life. There is no electricity to use the elevator, to watch TV, or even to use the phone or heat the water. People are live minute by minute, running down the stairs to the basement for shelter, and feel lucky if they have stored some bread bought at the bakery during a lull in the bombing.

In the middle of this confusion, a lady is screaming in the basement: "I forgot, I forgot!" "What did you forget?" people around her ask her. But she keeps screaming, "I forgot, I forgot!" all the while tearing her hair by the roots and slapping her cheeks. Meanwhile, the building seems to be swaying left and right from the vibrations of exploding shells all around our neighborhood. Every one is feeling his heart breaking into pieces and his very veins buzzing unbearably, because the kind of rocket that is raining uses a chain of explosions close-packed together, of the type called *ʿanqudiyya* or cluster-bomb in Arabic.

The overall feeling is that the moment of death has come. Everyone reaches for their children and covers them with their arms, so that they may be taken with them and not leave them alone in death. At that moment, love of mothers for their children shone. So did love of fathers, husbands and wives, and all family members who counted together the moments that remained before they would leave this life. Everyone recited the prayers that he or she knew, busy with his or her own person, engaged in private supplication to God for salvation. The whispering and the chanting of prayer was the only sound other than the sound of exploding shells above us. Nothing broke the gloom of this small basement except a few candles lit here and there, giving us hope like islands of light in a sea of darkness.

The intensity of the bombing reaches its peak. The shells have reached us, and we are all going to be shattered to pieces. The building is crumbling like cardboard, and the stones and bricks are heard falling around the streets of the neighborhood, like hail on the head of people on a winter day. In the middle of this rain of stones over human heads, the lady's voice also reached its peak, and she was now heard screaming: "Please! Let someone help my child! Someone help him! He is dying! He has been killed!" But no-one can see who she is referring to, and no-one is able to help her.

My sister took some cool water and tried to bring the lady to her senses by throwing water on her face, at the same time she kept asking where her child was so that she could be rescued." My sister called me: "Come and help me with her." I came and helped, and she said: "Please! I forgot my daughter. "Where? "In the tenth floor, in our apartment." My face turned pale. I looked into my sister's eyes, interrogating her without speaking, but she understood that I was telling her: "There might no longer be a tenth floor, or a fifth floor, or even a ground floor over us! Can we even get out of this basement alive?" People huddled around us, and we began to hear knocks on the metal door of the basement. The door was open from outside, three men and two ladies rushed in, shouting to us: "Close it behind us, close it quickly!" They had come at high speed with their car, not knowing where to go until they glimpsed the basement entrance to our shelter. They had jumped out of their car and rushed in for cover. We gave them some water and tried to calm them down from the shock of what they had seen outside. Their faces and clothes were covered with blood as they had been helping transport the wounded and the dead in their car.

One of the newcomers said: "The streets are littered with the dead. We don't know who to pick up anymore. Complete buildings have been razed to the ground. It is horror, disaster! I looked in turn at the first screaming lady, and then at the lady who was speaking. I said:

"What about our building?"

"Which building do you mean?"

"This building, our building!"

All five newcomers cried out in a confused clamor:

"There is nothing left outside, there is no more building! We saw a ruin of four or five floors' height, that's all that's left!"

When the first lady heard this, we thought she was going to go mad or even fall dead. All turned to her with bated breaths, ready to catch her if she fell. But the contrary happened. She seemed to calm down all of a sudden, catching her breath and becoming firm, staring at a corner of the basement. Her face changed colors, from pale to pink, her eyes became full of light, even smiling, and her mouth fell gaping as she said in a whisper:

"O my God -- O my God -- O my God!"

Everyone forgot about the shelling. We became oblivious to the apocalyptic thunder outside; instead, there was silence all around us. Every heart suddenly felt this great peace covering us all around, like a big mantle of quiet and rest, taking us to a different place in a short moment. Everyone stared in the direction of the lady's stare, but no-one could see what she was seeing. She stammered:

"O my God! I can see your angels! I can see your helpers with their wings, helping my daughter, they came to help us!"

As soon as she pronounced the word "angel," everybody felt a cool breeze, fragrant with an inexpressible perfume of flowers and fresh scents, covering the sulfuric smoke that had been drifting in from outside.

The candles went out. An immense light appeared, filling the whole basement and seemingly expanding it infinitely. Everyone froze in their place, unable to detach their gaze from this great cloud of light, staring at the light without the slightest strain, although it seemed many times as intense as the sun itself! Tongues were muted. No-one breathed. An immense peace descended, and all the suffering and shelling of the last few hours was forgotten.

The lady was now in a state of happiness, and all anxiety had disappeared from her. "Angels are saving my daughter." She kept repeating this, despite the apparent incongruity of her phrase, because everyone had thought that the building above us had been reduced to rubble and all the lives of those still in it, lost. Yet everyone now firmly believed that anything could happen because of the state we had entered, although anyone hearing this from the outside would consider it nonsense that the lady's daughter could still be alive.

My sister looked at me silently begging for some kind of answer. I stared back, eyes wide open, as if telling her: "God is great, He can do anything, even send His guardian angels to heal the wounds of helpless people who supplicate Him." She understood, and the reflection of this message seemed to enter her heart in waves of spiritual energy, now overflowing her heart and reaching the hearts of others all around us. Everyone seemed aware of a special event happening to them, which they had never experienced before in their lives.

My sister had been suffering from cancer for several years. A gynecologist by profession, she understood more than anyone else the facts about cancer and the gravity of her situation. She had undergone surgery and many treatments of chemotherapy. Doctors had finally told her that she had but a few months left to live. She was now in pain at the thought of death knocking at her door and about to enter, in addition to the pains of the disease itself and its harrowing treatment.

She was looking at me as if trying to ask: "If this visitation is real -- if it is happening that that woman's child is being helped by an angel, and we are seeing something to prove it -- why doesn't the

same angel also touch me with his miraculous healing, and save me as other people are being saved?" I understood all this in a moment, and we had not exchanged a single syllable.

I felt then and there that my sister was desperately asking, with all her heart, for help. She was trying to reach for the robe of an angel, clutching it in a last-minute attempt to be saved, as if this precious moment might not be repeated again in her lifetime. Something amazing and unexpected immediately followed this silent dialogue: my sister was now gazing at the corner of the basement with the same stare that we had seen on the face of the woman who was missing her daughter. My sister's tongue began to move and stammer involuntarily: "My brother, my brother, an angel is coming towards me! O my God, O my God!" Everyone stared but no-one could see, as the angel was visible only to her, as it had previously been visible only to the woman. Yet the light in the room seemed to multiply again and again.

My sister screamed: "He is healing me! The angel is healing me!!" Then she fainted. Everyone was in a dilemma, wondering who to help: the first lady or my sister? But no-one moved, as we were all frozen in our respective places and unable to take it all in other than to say: "God is great." In the middle of this state of confusion and spiritual wonderment, everyone heard a distinct knock on the small metal door of the basement. Yet no-one could move from his place, afraid to lose this state of ecstasy and return to the world of bombs, the noises of war, the smells of fire and gunpowder, and the sight of the dead and wounded.

Each one of us felt responsible for opening the door, and yet legs seemed pinned in their places and no-one was moving. Among all these people, two children broke loose from their parents' arms, a boy and a girl, and ran toward the basement door. The parents screamed: "Come back, come back!" but the children were answering: "Angels, angels!" All eyes were on the children, and the parents were unable to move even one inch from their places to catch their children.

Everyone's heart stopped at the thought that the children might go out and be hurt by the shelling. Amazement grew tenfold at a new sight: the children were no longer walking on the ground, their feet were now raised one inch above the ground, and they were walking on thin air! Their parents lost their voices and were now questioning their senses. The children took over, as if pitying their parents' loss for words, and said: "Mom, dad, angels are coming to our help. Don't be afraid. They will deliver us."

The children must have taken but a moment to reach the door; for everyone else, however, it seemed like a year. What was happening with the children? Were they even the same children anymore, or were they angels in the disguise of children? Who was knocking at the door? As the children were approaching the door, we did not seem to hear knocks anymore, but musical sounds charming our ears and flowing into the air. Wonder, confusion, expectation, suspense: the first lady and her daughter, my sister's sight and her loss of consciousness, the silence, the light, the fragrance surrounding us, the knocking at the door, the children floating on the air and calmly announcing the presence of angels, all this seemed too much for us to understand.

For all its strangeness, everything we had seen so far belonged to the three dimensions; we apprehended it with the senses of our physical bodies, or at least tried. Everyone felt that what lay behind the door, however, was going to be completely different and unprecedented and unimaginable. It must surely be from a fourth dimension, a door to Paradise, an interaction with the heavenly world itself, not only with one or two of its inhabitants or with the elements of fragrance and sound.

In less than one second of the children's time they reached the door. Without their touching it, it opened by itself in front of them. We could see nothing through the door: no stairs leading to the street, no stone structure, not even ruins, nothing but an immense light. That light poured into the basement, sending in waves and waves of a visible energy carrying with it effects that reached the hearts; for we all felt a great effulgence of love and utter happiness in our hearts, a love we had never felt before in our lives. It did not equal even the most intense raptures of our adolescence.

We were in a trance. The two children vanished in the light, no longer to be seen. All eyes were transfixed, casting impossible gazes at the disappearing children, but unable to follow them into the light. The union of the children with the light caused the light to change colors, like a radiant rainbow, and affected our states as well, as if we were now seeing the children move into paradise with the eyes of our hearts rather than those of our heads.

A brief moment passed. The light was still there. Two children had gone into it, but now three were returning. They were holding hands. They seemed to saunter out of the fourth dimension of Paradise back into our third dimension..

The children looked airy and subtle, seemingly translucid, as if they were now angelic beings. Their own light kept changing like the light that was coming through the door. An innocent gesture, typical of children, assured us that it was them: they were holding hands and moving in a circle, chanting a rhyme:

"We are the angels, we are the guardians,

We are those who love you and care for you."

Everyone heaved a sigh of relief and joy. We turned to each other gleefully, relishing both the sound and the meaning of that music carried by the children's voices. It was as if a new life had been opened to us in that basement, especially for the parents of the children. They had been trying to move from their places and to run and hug their children, but their efforts were in vain: they could not move. They were stuck in their places like stone statues.

As the light began to diminish little by little, the people began to feel that their powers of movement were coming back to them.

The state of ecstasy was lessening and abating in our bodies and our hearts. The children were slowing down in their caroling. They turned towards their parents and began to make their way back to them. All of us were looked at the third child, a little girl who jumped into the basement and ran to the lady who had been crying at first. We understood that this was the daughter she had been worried about for leaving her on the tenth floor of the building.

Everyone had forgotten about my still-unconscious sister, including myself, instead looking at the children and expecting to hear from them some description of what they had seen. The joy of the parents cannot be described. The lady of the tenth floor who had thought that her child was lost with the rest of the building, now was seeing her running towards her and holding her in her arms, and she had not even forgotten to bring her Barbie doll with her! The mother was hugging her child, kissing her, and mumbling unintelligible words of thanks and prayers, unable for emotion to speak coherently.

During that joyful event, some other people and I were trying to reanimate my sister after we ourselves had just regained our normal state of consciousness. Others, however, were asking the little girl to tell how she had managed to come unscathed from the rubble and destruction outside. I was losing nothing of the many questions that were beginning to burst out from every mouth, pricking up my ears to hear any answer when it came. At the same time I was throwing some cologne water on my sister's face and tapping it lightly, comforting her back to health.

The little girl was speaking in a mixed state of happiness and fear: she was happy because of what she had seen in the world of angels, and she was afraid from the intensity and emotion of the people's questioning that had suddenly erupted around her. She was surprised at their agitation and at the reaction of her mother, not realizing what all the fuss was about; she had just been visiting with her friends, the angels, and now here she was. What about the tenth floor? What about your room? But the little girl only said: "Mom, why are you crying? Why are you kissing me as if you had not seen

me for a week?" The mother kept hugging her dear child, continuing her muted, grateful prayers.

The little girl began to hug her Barbie doll, exactly as her own mother was hugging her. Each feared the loss of the little baby whom she held dear: the mother feared for her little daughter, the daughter feared for her little Barbie doll.

The little girl said: "I was in my bed when I felt someone touching me and calling me. I thought it was mom, but I never felt myself carried up and held that way before! I opened my eyes and I smelled a very nice breeze filling my room. I saw a lady coming to me, accompanied by an angel. Where my room had been there was now a great space without end and without beginning. The lady took me by the hand, and the angel carried both of us. I was about to cry, and the lady said to me: 'Why are you crying, sweetheart?' I said: 'I forgot Barbie.' The lady said: 'No, she is here with you, look under your arm.' I looked, and I found that my Barbie was with me. Then I looked around and began to shout: 'Where is my mother? What is happening? Where are you taking me?' And they said: 'We are taking you to your mother. We are your guardian angels.' Then I met the two children who were waiting for me in the hallway, where everything was light. The angels taught us a song and we began to play with them and go around. It was so nice! Then they told us that we had to go back to our parents and we came here."

The children did not seem to realize the extraordinary nature of the little girl's account, and of their entire experience of the last hour. We looked at them, then looked at each other in amazement and disbelief. Surely other people had to be told all this. Would they believe us? We did not wish the moment to end. We wanted to hear more. All these thoughts came to us at the same time, and above the din of these reflections one clear thought emerged and imposed itself: angels had come to our rescue and had brought us this precious moment of relief and mercy.

We had not forgotten the one among us who was lying on the ground: my sister. She was slowly coming to, and looked around her to see if the vision was still present. Someone handed me a cup of water with some drops of rose water in it. I gave the glass to my sister to moisten her tongue and quiet her nerves. She was at first unable to relate anything of what had happened to her. She drank some more water and slowly took in the surroundings, feeling more secure and happy as she came to understand the reunion scene that was taking place before her.

My sister then looked at me, and I understood from her eyes that she was ready to tell me what had happened to her and what she had observed under the touch of the angelic vision she had experienced. Everyone became quiet again, wanting to hear her story as well. It seemed like the soldier's rest after the excitement of battle. If someone had dropped a needle on the floor you could have heard it, although the fighting was still going on outside. Inside, the atmosphere of peace and happiness had disconnected us completely from the bedlam of war.

As she prepared to speak, everyone began to anticipate great news of joy and deliverance from her as well, although they had not heard anything yet. She said: "Praise God! He heals and He forgives. As soon as you saw me fainting, I woke up somewhere else and was looking at everyone. I felt like a patient undergoing anesthesia, but the 'going under' was spiritual. The angels were operating on me. I saw three of them: one on my right side, one on my left, and one above me. The latter one said to me: 'We are the healing angels, and we came to help you by God's permission. Nothing prevents us from curing anyone who seeks our help, and here we are!'"

"They were holding my hands on my two sides, and I felt a state of peace in my whole body. It made me feel light and relaxed. The familiar pain of many years of cancer treatment had left me. Then the angel above me showed me a staff of light which he was holding in his hand. He told me: 'There are points in the human body which, if anyone touches them, will cause healing in the entire body. I am going to touch them with this needle of light.' He proceeded to direct his staff at several points over my body, touching one cell-point each time and healing the cells that corresponded to it. 'These dead cells are given life another time through this touch,' he said."

"The operation extended over my entire body. I was able to count 365 different points to which he turned his staff. The angel said to me: 'Each point represents a day of the year. If you keep your body balanced through that year, all your years will be balanced, and your life's age will be balanced as well.'"

We had all been overwhelmed by the events that had happened, and now the secret knowledge which had been revealed to us added to our amazement. My sister continued: "The angel advised me that I must follow a certain diet which I must not leave for the rest of my life. In order to balance these life-points in the body, I must drink every day, in the early morning, before eating or drinking anything, a small cup of onion juice which will revive the dead cells that the cancer thrives upon to extend over the body. The angel said that this recipe should be followed by all who suffer from cancer."

We continued to listen to my sister's account of her angelic encounter, drinking in the many details which confirmed and reinforced the veracity of her experience in the light of the little girl's parallel journey. Each person in the basement was transformed that day. What irony that the day which had begun as one of the darkest in our lives, now seemed destined to be remembered as a day of special joy and blessing, to be recounted for a long time to come as one of the best in our lives! The people continued to recount their feelings and hear each other's impressions, seemingly for hours. When the excitement abated, three hours had passed, and a lull had replaced the chaos of indiscriminate shelling outside. Everybody prepared to leave the shelter and go back, as much as possible, to the normalcy of daily life.

When we came out we saw the extent of the damage. We realized that we had also been part of the angel's miraculous deed, as we had been spared and our basement protected from the bombing which had reached every spot around it. We left the city and made our way to my brother's house in the North of the country. There we healed our wounds and rested for a while. My sister faithfully followed the angel's recipe. After three months, she went back to her doctors at the American University of Beirut. To everyone's surprise, there was no trace of cancer left in her entire body. No-one could explain what had taken place and the doctors were mind-boggled. They did not even know how to trace the process of healing and found themselves unable either to describe it or to duplicate it. Of course, they took the causes of healing forwarded by my sister, the angel's operation and the recipe with a big grain of salt, although she was like them, a medical doctor. "Our colleague has had great luck," they said, "and is under the emotional stress of an unexpected, miraculous recovery." Miraculous it was, but more literally so than they could possibly imagine.

Angels
Who Chant
in Heaven

A friend of mine who had spent some time working in a city far from his wife and daughter suddenly felt a need to leave everything and visit them. He went to his room, sat down, and began writing a letter to his employer to ask for permission to absent himself from work. He then submitted the letter to the secretary, and expected to receive the permission after two or three days had passed, as was usual in such cases. He waited impatiently, but when the letter came back, it said that he could not take holidays at that time. He could not call his wife, as there were no telephones available in the area where they lived. He came back to his house, took a shower, and put a log in the fireplace. It was a snowy day. He sat and began to meditate, looking at the fire flickering from time to time. After a while he began to see the images of the members of his family moving with the movement of the flames. In spirit he began to visit them, and saw himself greeting them one by one.

His vision was rudely interrupted by heavy knocks at the door. At first he paid no attention to them and tried to concentrate on the dancing flames. The knocks continued. He regretfully left his wife and daughter and came out of his pleasant reverie. Getting up slowly, he went to the door and opened it. There was no-one. He looked around: nothing but snow covering everything, and continuing to fall. He closed the door, but as he was making his way back to the couch he heard another knock on the door. He went back and opened it, but again there was no one there. He wondered what was happening and who it could be that was knocking on the door. Is someone playing with me, he thought, or am I imagining things? Could this be related to the angel I was reading about yesterday? The third time, he heard harder knocks, and this time he jumped up and ran to the door. He opened it in the hope to catch whatever he would see behind the door, as he was beginning to suspect the presence of a special power. When he saw what was there he experienced a great shock. A cloud of light was hovering three feet in front of him, covering everything within sight. Inside it, a face of inexpressible beauty was staring at him. Was it the face of a woman, a man, a child, or even a human being? All he could think at that time was that this was certainly an angel. He heard a voice that shook his heart to the core with emotion and love. The voice said:

*God is Most generous.*
*He calls us to His presence and gives us courage.*
*He returns goodness for our indifference.*
*He covers ours faults with His forgiveness,*
*And changes the sadness in our hearts to light.*
*We have become used to His benevolence*
*Which never leaves us.*

Then the face looked at him with an expression of indescribable compassion and said: "I will be the messenger of your heart to your family. I shall inform them of your yearning for them. Tomorrow they will be on their way to you." After speaking, the light seemed to increase a little bit, then everything disappeared and nothing remained except snow falling softly on the ground. No footsteps. It was night. The man looked up and down, right and left, but he could see nothing anymore. He wore nothing on top of his flannel shirt but was insensitive to the cold. Every hair on his body was standing on end, and his heart was beating faster than it had ever beaten before. He was in a state of excitement and pleasure he had never felt in his life. What was happening to him? The room had disappeared, the fire had disappeared, the couch, the tables, the grandfather clock, the mirror, everything had disappeared and nothing was there except the memory of that angel, engraved within the pupils of his eyes and on his heart. This state of ecstasy remained with him the whole night.

When morning came and the darkness disappeared, his state abated little by little. When the sun had completely risen, it had left him completely. He asked himself: "Was that a dream? Did I hallucinate? Or is this the angelic visitations that they are talking so much about?" He mentally reviewed the stories about angels he had heard about or read, but in none of these stories could he recall anything even remotely resembling what he had seen. He struggled with himself between the states of belief and unbelief, unable to admit without reservation the truth of what he had seen. Finally he said to himself: "If that was an angel, then my wife and children are coming today."

That day he went to work and everything seemed to go on as usual. He was excited, and felt that the day was lasting forever. He wanted the day to finish and go home to check if what had happened was real or not. When five o'clock came, he was the first to pack his things and leave. As he reached home, to his surprise, he saw his wife and child in the distance, standing at the doorstep. He ran to them in a daze, asking himself a thousand questions at the same time. They were greeting him happily and hugging him.

He was dumbfounded. Can this be possible? Are they real, or am I hallucinating? He heard the voice of his little girl saying to him: "Daddy, it's us, the angel brought us; me and mom!!" He took her in his arms and turned to his wife. He realized that he had been indeed visited by an angel. In his heart everything that he had known before had crumbled and been replaced with a new understanding about the reality of this world. Angels were present among human beings and exerted their powers over worldly events to help them. He took his wife into his arms and tried to open the door, but his hand was shaking. His wife said: "Dear, what is troubling you? Why are you shaking so much?" He said: "Later, later, I'll tell you about it." She took the keys from his hand and opened the door.

"What inspired you to come at this time?" he asked.

She answered:

"I was reading a story to our daughter yesterday, and I was telling her about the angels who chanted in heaven. She asked me what these were, and I was trying to explain the chanting of the angels. Suddenly we began to hear a wonderful melody filling the room. We saw a light, and inside it a little girl just like ours, who said: 'I am the chanting angel!' Our daughter asked me if I could see what she was seeing and I reassured her that I was. She asked: 'Angel,

where is my dad?' The angel said: 'He is waiting for you and he is sending his love.' I could not believe this was happening, but here was our little child telling me that it was all true! And so we decided to come, and here we are!"

"They were holding my hands on my two sides, and I felt a state of peace in my whole body. It made me feel light and relaxed. The familiar pain of many years of cancer treatment had left me. Then the angel above me showed me a staff of light which he was holding in his hand. He told me: 'There are points in the human body which, if anyone touches them, will cause healing in the entire body. I am going to touch them with this needle of light.' He proceeded to direct his staff at several points over my body, touching one cell-point each time and healing the cells that corresponded to it. 'These dead cells are given life another time through this touch,' he said."

"The operation extended over my entire body. I was able to count 365 different points to which he turned his staff. The angel said to me: 'Each point represents a day of the year. If you keep your body balanced through that year, all your years will be balanced, and your life's age will be balanced as well.'"

We had all been overwhelmed by the events that had happened, and now the secret knowledge which had been revealed to us added to our amazement. My sister continued: "The angel advised me that I must follow a certain diet which I must not leave for the rest of my life. In order to balance these life-points in the body, I must drink every day, in the early morning, before eating or drinking anything, a small cup of onion juice which will revive the dead cells that the cancer thrives upon to extend over the body. The angel said that this recipe should be followed by all who suffer from cancer."

We continued to listen to my sister's account of her angelic encounter, drinking in the many details which confirmed and reinforced the veracity of her experience in the light of the little girl's parallel journey. Each person in the basement was transformed that day. What irony that the day which had begun as one of the darkest in our lives, now seemed destined to be remembered as a day of special joy and blessing, to be recounted for a long time to come as one of the best in our lives! The people continued to recount their feelings and hear each other's impressions, seemingly for hours. When the excitement abated, three hours had passed, and a lull had replaced the chaos of indiscriminate shelling outside. Everybody prepared to leave the shelter and go back, as much as possible, to the normalcy of daily life.

When we came out we saw the extent of the damage. We realized that we had also been part of the angel's miraculous deed, as we had been spared and our basement protected from the bombing which had reached every spot around it. We left the city and made our way to my brother's house in the North of the country. There we healed our wounds and rested for a while. My sister faithfully followed the angel's recipe. After three months, she went back to her doctors at the American University of Beirut. To everyone's surprise, there was no trace of cancer left in her entire body. No-one could explain what had taken place and the doctors were mind-boggled. They did not even know how to trace the process of healing and found themselves unable either to describe it or to duplicate it. Of course, they took the causes of healing forwarded by my sister, the angel's operation and the recipe with a big grain of salt, although she was like them a medical doctor. "Our colleague has had great luck," they said, "and is under the emotional stress of an unexpected, miraculous recovery." Miraculous it was, but more literally so than they could possibly imagine.

Angels
Guide to
Safety

The year is 1980. It was Saturday, July 7. I had just returned from overseas to my home in Beirut, Lebanon, the city known as "Switzerland of the Middle East." When the plane landed in Beirut Airport, it was an emergency landing because of the war going on at that time. I tried to contact my brother to pick me up. It was impossible because all telephone lines had been put out of commission. People were rushing through the customs and immigration controls. It was difficult to find an officer available to stamp your passport. Everyone was running for his own dear life. You felt that you might die at any moment. I looked around for a taxi, but found no-one willing to go up north, where I lived. Beirut was divided into two sides, and you could not go up north except by crossing from one side to the other, over the infamous Green Line, which no-one felt bold enough to do on that particular day.

A few hours passed. The airport and the streets around it were deserted, except for one couple and their small child who had travelled on the same plane as me. They were sitting in the cafeteria where they could not even find a cup of water for their baby. They had run into the same problem: no-one was found to take them to Tripoli which was about two hours from the airport by car.

I sat not far from the stranded family. We could hear the cacophony of crashing shells, less than a mile away on the coast-line. All of us were wondering how to reach home that day. I went into a state of prayer and meditation. I remembered my master, and I asked for help from God through the intercession of my master. Another hour went by. Night was falling. We could see the red sun about to disappear below the horizon.

Suddenly, I saw a car speeding towards the airport and approaching the parking lot outside the cafeteria window. It seemed to be racing as if trying to escape some terrible pursuers. It screeched to a halt outside the main door, and a high-ranking officer of the Lebanese Army dashed out of it. He was the officer responsible for the airport. From a distance I wondered whether I knew that person, as he seemed familiar to me. As he approached I realized this was one of the followers of my master, who therefore belonged to the same spiritual group as I.

When the officer saw me, he expressed less surprise than I did, and I felt that he was hiding something in his heart. We hugged each other. He asked:

"What are you doing here?"

"I arrived today. I am waiting for a car to take me home. What about you, what are you doing here?"

"I don't have time to answer you quickly right now; get your luggage and put it in the car."

I brought my luggage as he instructed and we got into the car. He started the car again and put in reverse. I looked at the stranded couple and their little child.

When they saw us leaving, they seemed to lose hope, as if resigned for impending disaster. That had terrified me, and my friend was also afraid of the idea of being stranded in that forlorn place. In the car, I felt as if the child was sending us a message: "All of us are innocent people. God created us to live in peace and happiness in this lovely world, extending our hands to each other as human beings. I want to enjoy this life as much as you, and play under the trees that rise up towards heaven, and hear the birds, and watch the waves breaking on the sea-shore. I don't want to die!" When I seemed to hear the child's appeal in my heart, tears came to my eyes and I thought: "Am I leaving behind this family at night, with no-one taking care of them?"

The car began to back up, but something was holding the both of us. I said:

"I cannot go without them."

"Let us save our souls! Everyone is finding death on his way nowadays. They are shelling each other like mad."

"I cannot go without them. We have to take them with us."

"All right. Let us get them."

I waved with my hand for them to come. They thought I was giving them a farewell gesture! In their depressed state, they could not even imagine that I was inviting them to get in. The child began to cry. All the while we were hearing the sound of the shelling approaching our area.

I got down from the car with my friend. We ran to them and screamed: "Come on!" They got on their feet, electrified by the sudden hope for salvation. They were practically dancing with joy as we helped them carry their luggage to the car. We scrambled into the car again and screeched away, heading for the north.

I asked my friend a second time how he knew that I was at the airport. Again, he said: "Later. We have to decide which way to take right now. Shall we take the two-hour trip by the sea-shore, or go the other way around, through the mountains, ten thousand feet above sea-level through the Cedars and then down to Tripoli? It would take us twelve hours. There is no shelling on that road, but at this hour, any armed group might rob us, kill us, take the car and go!"

We were in the middle of this dilemma when the little girl said out of nowhere: "I want to see the sea-shore. I don't want to go through the mountains. Please, uncle, take us to the seashore." Her father said: "And why do you want to go the seashore?" The child answered: "Because the angel told me so." The father was in no mood to hear about angels. However, the child's words rang like thunder in my ears. It was as if the angel had spoken to the child in order to direct the mature ones. I said to my friend on the spot:

"Let us go the sea-shore."

"Why did you reach such a quick decision?"

"Because I have experience with the angels. The lives of my master, of all our masters, of the Prophet, and of all prophets, are full of illustrations of this."

These words were like the key that opened my friend's heart and his lips. He said:

> "I was afraid you would think I am crazy when you were asking me what brought me to the airport. Do you know what brought me to the airport?"
>
> "I don't know, but I can guess that something has led you here despite your will and against your intentions. It couldn't have been me, because I didn't call you. The phones are out. I didn't write you either: there is no post. However, you are here!"
>
> "I was busy in my office with paperwork related to airport security. I was writing work schedules for the officers in downtown Beirut. I was sitting alone. I heard a voice out of the blue. It seemed to come from every corner of the room, but it was garbled. I looked around me. There was no-one. I opened the door. No-one in the hallway either. I closed the door and went back in. Imagine me, a general in the army, trained for warfare, prepared for death at the hands of a terrorist attack, and I was now wondering about voices. After I sat, I heard the voice again. Again I got up and looked everywhere, even out in the street but it was deserted."
>
> "I left the paperwork and listened. I tried to muster all my attention and place it in my ears, to check if I was really hearing something and from where it came. This time instead of hearing something, I saw the walls of the room recede until they seemed to disappear! I rubbed my eyes: am I hallucinating now? I reached for the pot of coffee behind the

desk and poured myself two cups. But even after I had drunk the coffee the vision was still there. I took the bottle of water next to the coffee-pot and I poured it on top of my head. I did not change a thing. I felt an intense heat. I realized that something extraordinary was happening to me."

"The moment that this thought of acceptance dawned upon me in my heart, it was as if I had used the secret code permitting me to enter a further state of understanding or vision. I began to understand that what I was experiencing was real, and not an imagined occurrence or a hallucination."

The feeling inside the car had changed from that of a dangerous trip to that of a mysterious story. Shells were falling all around us. In front of us cars were stopping and people were looking for shelter. Buildings were on fire. From the other end of the street another car was rushing towards us, and when they reached our level they shouted: "Move quickly, this is a war zone!" Great was our surprise to see that the driver of that car was smiling, although he was warning us about great impending danger. We wondered why he seemed so happy. Even more strangely, his face shone brightly and seemed to light everything around us.

My friend dispelled our wonder and exclaimed: "This is the same light and the same face that I saw in my office! He is the one who visited me!" This gave my friend the much-needed sign that he was on the right track. He continued on his way through the coastal highway towards the Green Line that cut the center of the city, and he continued his story.

"When I realized that I was not imagining things, I began to see a light that was taking over the whole room, and replacing everything in it with a great white cloud. In the middle of this cloud I saw an angel that resembled that shining man who smiled in the car that just passed us, but the angel was standing. In his hand he was carrying a white bird and he addressed me in those words: 'You have to go to the airport.'

> I was unable to respond to him because I was too overwhelmed to speak. I was unable to ask for further confirmation that this was a message for me. It was clear enough: something had come to me and instructed me to go to the airport. At the same time, it was impossible for me to say: 'I cannot go because there is too much shelling.' Immediately as I was thinking of these objections, the vision would repeat: 'Go to the airport.' He repeated this order three times. Finally I gave in and decided to go. I left everything and here I am."

Everybody in the car was happy after hearing this story and yet we were afraid of what lay ahead. We were happy to know that an angel had reunited us and yet we were afraid at the prospect of crossing the war-zone. Our faith was high nevertheless because we had seen three signs: first, my friend had come on orders from an angel; second, the child had mentioned the message of an angel to him; and third, the same angel who had spoken to my friend had passed by us in a car and told us to move quickly.

We were about to reach the Green Line, where the shelling and shooting were at their most intense. Warriors from every side were scrambling everywhere. These were unprincipled people who killed without the slightest provocation. They delighted even in shooting at a bird if they could only sight one. My friend stepped on the gas pedal. The couple in the back seat were shouting: "Please! they are looking at us! They are going to kill us!" But the little girl exclaimed: "No, no! Mom, dad, don't you see the angels protecting us? They are everywhere, chaining all the armed people! The warriors cannot move! They are like mummies wrapped in their chains, without movement!"

My friend and I felt a renewed burst of confidence when we heard the little girl's words. It was as if we were inside a plane flying between the clouds; no-one could see the plane except a radar detector. The car was moving, crossing the streets as if veiled from everyone's eyes. We were hearing and seeing both sides fighting with

each other, but no-one cared about us nor even noticed our presence. Only the angels were seeing us and guiding us, as the radar guides the airplane flying blindly in the middle of a storm.

We soon found ourselves on the other side. We had crossed safely and nothing had happened to us. We found ourselves in a state of happiness and relief that made the hair on our bodies stand on end. Had we really made it safely through, the only car to pass the Green Line at that time? The child kept repeating: "The angels saved us, the angels saved us!"

We continued on our way, heading north for Tripoli. It was not over yet. The way was full of other dangers. The militias and the different parties had their soldiers posted all along the road, and we had to face them also, as we had faced the snipers and the shells. But the confidence the angels had placed in our hearts had grown to the extent that we felt sure of ourselves. We drew comfort from the sweet voice of our youngest passenger, who never stopped saying "angels are with us!"

After a half hour of driving safely in the dead of the night, we saw a checkpoint one mile ahead of us. Many cars had been stopped and pulled to the side. People were being taken away. My friend slowed down. He began to feel afraid, although he was an army general. It was impossible to change our way and go back, as this was the only way available to us. We had no alternative but to continue. As we were approaching, we could see the soldiers put handcuffs on people, not differentiating between men and women, and even slapping them on their faces and pushing them. Even children were not safe from their violence. We could hear many children screaming for their parents. Without fear of reprisal and without shame, the soldiers were kicking them and shoving them with their boots, showing no pity.

The parents of the little girl tried to hide their child under the seat, ordering her to huddle between their legs. But the little girl said:

"Why are you afraid, don't you see that the angels are coming with us? Look at all of them, some by the windshield, some holding the handle of the car doors, and others sitting at the back on top of the trunk!"

We all felt an immense relief . There was hope yet that we would pass that checkpoint unharmed. When we arrived, my friend slowed down and prepared to stop. But no-one was paying any attention to us. It was as if we did not exist on this earth. My friend waited for a few moments lest they should shoot at us if we moved. No-one was paying any attention. The little girl jumped out of the back seat and spoke to the driver, saying: "Uncle, move, don't wait! They will never see us, because the angels are covering us."

My friend felt encouraged to move, and he stepped on the gas pedal. He crossed the checkpoint and soon it was a distant blur behind us, its people continuing to stop the cars that came behind. We had apparently changed into ghosts! An hour later, we reached Tripoli safe and sound. It was just after midnight. And that is how we were saved from fear and destruction, as Jonah had been brought out safe and sound from the belly of the whale.

Zahra
and the
Angels of
Magic

The ways to God are infinite; their number according to the breaths of created beings. God has allowed even children and the illiterate to have knowledge of Him. He brings out a teaching for sincere believers from everything in creation. He produces instruction sometimes even from what is apparently devoid of teaching or seems foolish and contradictory to wisdom. A pious saint was once asked: "From where did you learn your angelic manners?" He replied: "From the enemies of angels who are devoid of angelic manners."

God has created the angels rank upon ordered rank, in hierarchies of light and sublime levels of unimaginable beauty. Their number cannot be counted, their perfections are beyond enumeration. Their knowledge is infinite. However, their rank before God is bestowed and never acquired. God, on the other hand, bestows a rank upon mankind which He permits mankind to acquire. That is: they may reach the rank after they step upon their lower soul and use it as a stairway to perfection. Because the angels have been created perfect and without egos, they have no stairway to use. Therefore, God has created them with the same perfection as they will have throughout their existence. Human beings are created in order to progress to the knowledge of God represented in the verse of the Holy Quran:

*And I did not create the jinn and human beings except to worship Me.*[61]

When God decided to create Adam, the holy and pure angels who are endowed by God with divine love felt pity for human beings whom they foresaw would shed blood on earth. They were concerned that mankind would never be able to know God the way that angels do. God answered them by alluding to the secret of the creation of human beings: for it is by their effort in this regard that they earn higher and higher rank among the angelic lights. In this, of

61 Surat adh-Dhariyat, 51:56

course, they are unlike the angels who obey God effortlessly and whose rank remains forever unchanged.

> *And when thy Lord said unto the angels: "Lo! I am about to place a viceroy in the earth," they said: "Wilt Thou place therein one who will do harm therein and will shed blood, while we, we hymn Thy praise and sanctify Thee?" He said: "Surely, I know that which ye know not."*[62]

To show the angels the exalted ranks of human beings, God asked who among them would go to the earth and live as mortal beings in order to experience the reality of the human condition directly. Two angels stepped forward: Harut and Marut.. The Quran relates:

> *And follow that which the devils falsely related against the kingdom of Solomon. Solomon disbelieved not; but the devils disbelieved, teaching mankind magic and that which was revealed to the two angels in Babel, Harut and Marut. Nor did they (the two angels) teach it to anyone till they had said: We are only a temptation, therefore disbelieve not in the guidance of God. And from these two angels people learned that by which they cause division between man and wife but they injure thereby no-one save by God's leave.*[63]

God sent them down into a city of believers; one was to act as a judge, while the other was to be a scholar. They lived, ate, and drank as mortal people during the day. At night, they returned to their heavenly stations by means of the Most Holy Name which had been vouchsafed to them on account of their angelic nature.

In that town lived a most beautiful woman by the name of Zahra (some say Anahid). She realized that Harut and Marut were not normal human beings, but rather angels who possessed a great secret. She resolved to obtain it no matter what it cost her. She invited the two angels to her house and made a feast for them. She

---

[62] Surat al-Baqara, 2:30

[63] Surat al-Baqara, 2:102

gave them the best of food and drink. Since the angels had been given a human lower soul, they were vulnerable and corruptible. Under the influence of wine and music their heads became light and they forgot that they were angels. They fell in love with Zahra-Anahid. When she asked them to show their true identity they revealed themselves, and they gave away the secret of the Most Holy Name. Zahra-Anahid immediately spoke the Name, and as soon as she had pronounced it, she flew off and disappeared from the face of the earth, and was never seen there again. It is said that the Lord of the Worlds forgave her, and set her as a star upon the firmament. It is called Zuhra (Venus) and rises in the sky in the early morning or evening.

As for the two angels who remained behind, they slowly recovered from their heedlessness. But when they tried to recite the secret Name they found that they could no longer escape their earthly forms. They were inextricably enmeshed in worldly existence. This is because for so short a moment they had exchanged the cloak of the remembrance of God for the cloak of the remembrance of the world. It was then that the realization of what had befallen dawned on them. Realizing the truth of God's word concerning human beings, they were amazed at the fortitude of prophets and saints who never lose glimpse of God for a second, even though they are human beings. When God saw that they repented, he said to them: "Now do you see the rank of mankind, and how much they are beloved to Me? If they decide to come to Me one hand-span, I shall come to them an arm-span; and if they walk to Me, I shall run to them; and if they remember Me, I shall remember them."

Harut and Marut remained on earth both as a lesson and a test to human beings. Would-be students of magic flock to them to be instructed, but they always meet them with the words: "We are only a temptation, so beware! Remember God, and don't disbelieve in him." They taught human beings all the esoteric arts and branches of "occult" knowledge: astrology, alchemy, numerology, the healing arts, and magic. They never give away their knowledge, however, without a warning to the would-be practitioner: if his heart is pure, he is safe, if not, he is in danger of losing himself among the lower beings of the earth, the jinn.

There are sixty verses mentioning magic (*sihr*) in the holy Quran. "Magical and enticing" are attributes of this-worldly life in the language of angels, prophets, and saints. In the prophetic tradition, eloquence and poetry are also described as possessing something "magical and enchanting." Found in their most intense manifestations, such arts attract audiences with something similar to spells. Music also contains a magic touch which sways the senses and takes one to a dimension of elation or euphoria. Such things may be considered a constructive sort of magic. In this guise, it benefits mankind. On the other hand, there is another magic that separates husband and wife, friends, brothers and sisters, or that brings about bad events for others. This kind of magic is unacceptable because of its destructiveness.

Magic may be equally constructive and destructive when it comes to the mind. This duality of magic is reflected in the story of the two angels who are both men and angels, whose human dimension is to forget and whose angelic dimension is to remind and teach. People who deal in psychic forces nowadays are similarly divided into two groups. There are those who bring people exclusively material benefits and do not stop them from harming others. These must be avoided. They are a danger to themselves and those who consult them. Then there are those who help people build up their lives in constructive and spiritual ways. The latter kind work for goodness and they enjoy the assistance of the angelic powers.

Urwa
and the
Angel of
Consolation

The angel of consolation follows the angel of tears. When the angel of tears touches someone's heart with his wing, that person begins to weep.

One of the great saints, named ʿUrwa, grew very old and began to pray that God take Him back to Him and place Him among His beloved ones. One day, as he was making such a prayer by the graveside of St. John the Baptist in Damascus, he saw a very handsome young man coming to him, dressed in green and covered with blazing light. The young man smiled at ʿUrwa and said: "O my father, may God bless you! What prayer are you making?" Urwa told him: "O my son, may God have mercy on you! I am asking for a good end and a quick return to God for a goodly meeting with the loved ones. Who are you, my dear son?" He said: "I am the mercy of your Lord sent to console human beings. My name is Artiya'il and I am an angel. I was created to wipe away the sadness and pain from the breast of those beloved to God." Then the angel disappeared, and ʿUrwa's sadness was gone with him.

One day, the disciples of another great saint went among a certain tribe in Central Asia and weeks passed without them coming back. Their master was meditating one day with a heavy heart, worried that something might have happened to them. A green bird of Paradise came to his window and began to chant with a voice which wiped clean his heart from all sadness: "I am Artiya'il, I am the destroyer of sadness! I am the bringer of good news to the hearts of children and men and women young and old. I bring you news of your beloved ones." Later, the master said: "I knew Artiya'il would come, but I had to despair first!"

Artiya'il is the angel who allows people to return to their normal lives and free themselves from the pangs of depression and anxiety. These diseases of the soul are great tests which God sends to human beings to remind them that they should not run after material things and forget their angelic inheritance. Angels always remember God. If they stopped they would instantly cease to exist. Similarly, human beings need to remember the Creator of all that surrounds them in order to live happily in those surroundings.

> *Lo! verily the friends of God are those on whom fear cometh not, nor do they grieve... Theirs are good tidings in the life of the world and in the Hereafter.".*[64]

God ordered the angels to serve those who remember Him and fight those who forget Him. This is not to punish them but to help them and correct them. Babies and children cry when they are given bitter medicine. Grown-ups know their need for the angelic energies of goodness and beauty, and if they choose to ignore such a need, they are reminded of it through the medicine of depression. The latter is the effect of the "shock to the system" of those who forget God, the Creator of goodness and beauty.

The characteristic of an angelic nature is to be able to feed and sleep on the remembrance of God, whereas brute beasts are unable to feed on other than fodder or sleep without giving up their conscience. When human beings do this over a long period of time rust builds up on the heart. Depression settles in and melancholy finds a permanent home. That is why the Prophet said: "Everything has a polish, and the polish of hearts is the remembrance of God."

Depression is a sickness of heart and soul made possible only through heedlessness. A vigilant heart keeps belief and hope and trust posted at its gate as so many guardian angels. It never allows the darkness of depression and doubt to enter. Human hearts are a precious treasure. Many thieves lurk in the surrounding shadows looking to rob and plunder it. However, when the owner of the treasure is a friend of God, the treasure is well guarded. Its guardians are fed and paid with the currency of faith and remembrance. If there is no faith, there are no guardians; if no remembrance, no salary. Without guardians the palace doors lay open to what is unwanted.

---

[64] Surah Yunus, 10:62,64

Thieves will never go to an empty house. That is why the Holy Quran insists that:

*We verily did honor all the children of Adam*[65]

The explanation of that honor is the treasure which God deposited into the hearts of human beings.

Angels teach those among human beings who are able to connect with them never to be cheated and robbed of the angelic light of their hearts

[65] Surat an-Najm, 17:70

A
Saint
and
Archangel
Michael

God has created the Archangel Michael and put him in charge of nature, rain, snow, thunder, lightning, wind, and clouds. God has appointed a complete creation of angels to assist him and placed them under his command. These angels are countless and no-one other than God knows their number. God has given Michael power to see the entire span of the created universes at once, with no interference of other universes. He knows at all times where he has to send rain, wind, snow, and clouds without effort on his part.

The angels who assist him range in size from the hugest size imaginable to man to that of the smallest species living on this earth. They fill the entire atmosphere of every star and planet in every universe. Their praise to God can be heard by the other angels, by prophets, by saints, and by young children.

> *The thunder hymneth His praise and so do the angels for awe of Him. He launcheth the thunder-bolts and smiteth with them whom He will while they dispute in doubt concerning God, and He is mighty in wrath.*[66]

Michael is the angel of mercy which is another name for rain in Arabic. He is created from the light of God's attribute al-Rahman, "the Merciful." He was never seen smiling after hell was created. He was created before Gabriel.

Once upon a time, Gabriel and Michael visited the Prophet Muhammad, Peace be upon him. The latter had a toothstick in hand which he immediately handed to Gabriel, the angel who constantly brought him Revelation. Gabriel said: "O Muhammad! give it to the elder angel." The Prophet gave it to Michael.

The Prophet said: "God gave me two celestial assistants to help me deliver my Message: Gabriel and Michael." He used always to send for Gabriel and Michael concerning matters important to human beings.

---

[66] Surat ar-R'ad, 13:13

Gabriel is the caller to prayer *(muezzin)* in the heavens is and the prayer-leader *(imam)* is Michael. God created a house for Himself in Paradise (*al-Bayt al-Maʿmur*) to which the angels make pilgrimage every day five times. There, five prayer-services are held and every service is heralded by Gabriel and led by Michael. The angels all come with their lights and ornaments, their jewels and fragrances, chanting and praising God with their heavenly music. Some people on earth, especially children, are able to hear their voices. This sound gives them indescribable pleasure. Every angel chants and praises in a different language without clash or disharmony. All are pleading to God for mercy for human beings and asking Him to elevate the state of people so that they can hear and see these daily ceremonies. To reward the angels for their praise, for the sincerity of their intercession, and to show them the great extent of His mercy, God at every moment showers His mercy on human beings.

Until the time of the Prophet Noah the House of God existed on the face of the earth. People came from all over the world to walk ceremoniously around it the way pilgrims walk around the Kaʿba in Mecca today. When God set His face on sending the flood to drown the entire world, He ordered His angels to transport the Heavenly House up into the fourth heaven. It stands there until now with the angels walking continually around in solemn state. It was transformed into a Palace of Paradise. Its only remnant on earth is the Black Stone in the Holy Kaaba: it used to be white like the Palace it came from but has been clouded over blackened by the sins of mankind. It has been left on earth for the sake of remembrance. All who kiss it, it is as if they are kissing the right hand of God on earth.

While the angels carry the heavenly House up to heaven, their arms gird the building all around. By divine command they fall into a swoon and you would not know whether the angels are carrying the House or the House is carrying the angels, because the mere task of lifting up that sacred abode causes them to loses their senses. In the fourth heaven, God Almighty created a pulpit of green emerald inside the House. He increased the numbr of its doors to three. One door is

made of topaz, one of green beryl, and the last fashioned from red gold. He created a prayer-niche of white pearls. In front of it He made a dividing curtain of many different kinds of gems. Next, He raised up the minaret opposite the middle door of the House which is all of diamonds. In the weekly congregational prayer when the callers to prayers are mounting the minarets of the mosque, God orders the angel Gabriel to mount that minaret of diamond and to give the call to prayer, *adhan*. When the angels in all seven heavens hear his voice, they all congregate around the heavenly House in the fourth heavens.

Then the angel Michael mounts the pulpit and delivers the sermon. When the sermon ends, Michael descends and the angel Israfil leads the assembled angels in the performance of the weekly Friday prayer. After the last words of the prayer, Gabriel rises up and says to the angels, "O my brother angels! Bear witness to what I am about say . I am turning all the rewards God Almighty has written down for me to receive for performing the call to prayer today ovr the chidren of Adam—those who today have summoned people to prayer for the sake of the Almighty from all the minarets of the world." Then Michael gets up and says, "You assembly of angels! Bear witness to my words. The rewards of today's sermon I give as a gift to all those who have delivered a congregational sermon today on earth for the sake of God's pleasure." The Israfil also stands and addresses the angels, "O you angels of God! Bear witness that I am giving all the rewards that God Almighty has granted to me for leading the weekly prayer to every prayer-leader all over the globe who today have led the prayers."

All the other angels then join in and say, "God has created us to love human beings, to care for them and to send their hearts peace and happiness. We are at once their servants and their loving guardians. Everyone God has created in heavens and earth must bear witness that we donate the rewards of our prayer to all those who have prayed this prayer with good intent and purity of heart."

The Almighty Lord of heavens speaks to them and says, "O My beloved angels whom I created from the light of love and beauty; do you try to be more magnanimous than your Lord? Be aware that I, from the abundance of munificence, have decreed all My mercy for every servant in My court whose forehead bowed to Me and touched the ground today, and also for My servants who were not able to attend the congregational prayere for any excuse. I have given countless rewards to all who have honored this day and bowed their heads in reverent worship.

For every believer and his guardian angels God creates a tree in Paradise. Under its shadow one can walk for a hundred years. Its leaves are made of green emerald, its flowers from a rare diamond the color of gold. Its branches are of silk brocade. Its fruit has a heavenly taste and its sap is ginger and honey. Its trunk is sapphire, its soil musk, its grass saffron. From its roots, endless rivers spring and flow far and wide. At its foot stands a golden throne erected for its owner and adorned with all kinds of ornaments. God created special angels incomparable in beauty to attend that person. They stand at his service with faces radiant like moons with hair like strings of pearls. From their eyes emanate a light which opens countless windows to new creations fashioned just for him to behold.

Michael is the custodian of the Bell-Trees of Paradise. These are goldn trees with bells made of silver, out of each bell a light emanates a distance of one thousand years. Angels guide the inhabitants of Paradise by th light of those bells. That light allows them to see what no eye ever saw before, har what no ear heard no mind imagined before. God says to Michael, "Command the Bell-Tree to eexude from its branches a musk whose fragrance has never before been smelled to delight the inhabitants of Paradise. Michael orders a wind of sandalwood to emanate from under God's Throne and alight on these trees. It stirs the silver bells and causes such a swet sound to fill the air that if the people of the earth could listen, they would die instantly, so intense is the pleasure of it.

A saint enters a forest to fetch wood for his fire-place. It is winter and snowing hard. He sees a light in the middle of the forest. As he approaches that light he notices a man standing in its midst and he hears him reciting:

*Praise be to God Who causes hearts to believe*
*And makes tongues sweet who declare Him to be One*
*Who has made tyrants to bow down before Him,*
*And rolled up the globe grasped in His Hand*
*What was, and is, and is to come!*

The saint approached him and said, "Peace be upon you!"

"And upon you be peace, O saint of God!"

"Who are you and how do you know me?"

"The light of knowledge has illumined my heart. I know you with the certainty of the One Who sits on the Throne. My name is Michael, the angel."

"O Michael! When does God's servant reach the state of servanthood?"

"When the flag of guidance flutters above him and the light of protection encompasses him. At that time the state of perfection begins to appear in him."

"Tell me more about this state."

"God has servants sparing with speech, who often keeps vigil, and who dress themselves, in the garments of God's praise. Their tears are like rivers in God's Divine Presence; for their intercession on behalf of human beings is constant. Their food is only what they need to survive. They only sleep when fatigue overcomes them. They purify themselves until they reach a state of

nearness. When drawn near, God exchanges the garmeent of their poverty for that of His power and generosity. Whoever looks at thtem at that time will only see Him."

Then Michael recited:

*Gardens of Eden which they enter; along with all who do right by their fathers and thir helpmates and their seed. Thee angels enter unto them from every gate, saying: "Peace be unto your because you persevered." Ah, passing sweet will be the sequel of the heavenly Home.*[67]

Michael is assisted by an angel named Thunder, the custodian of the clouds, who sends them wherevere Michael wants them to go. He holds a huge stick with which he hits the clouds and moves them in whatever direction God wishes. The voice that we hear when it thunders is the sound of his praise. From that sound God creates angels escorting every drop of water that falls down to the earth and to the sea. These angels bring down the mercy of the rain the return to the Divine Presence. All are under Michael's order except the drops of snow. The angels who accompany the snow come down and remain among human beings to praise and glory God. Their rewards are written in the books of human beings and will be counted as their own on Judgment Day. That is why the snow is an even greater blessing than the rain.

The clouds have another custodian-angel named Annan, and the lightning yet another, Raphael. Raphael has four different faces; one heavenly, one human, one visible to the people of the graves, and one to those in the Hereafter.

A saint by the name of al-Ghujdawani once received a heavenly order conveyed by Michael to visit a certain mountain and to look upon a rock with the Divine Power with which God had endowed him. When he looked at the rock, thousands of springs

---

[67] Surat ar-Rʿad, 13:23-24

began to flow from it and formed a great waterfall. God said, "From every drop of this water, I am creating an angel whose praising shall continue until the Hereafter. Their reward will be written in the book of human beings. Your task, O Ghujdawani, will be to give a different name to each one of these angels and they will be under Michael's command."

By asking Ghujdawani to give names to millions of angels and enabling him to know them by their individual characteristics, God was showing that He was granting him an angelic power of cration and knowledge above that of His other servants. Such is the gift of God to His saints—He causes them to be like angels and boasts about them before the heavenly host.

A
Saint
& Angels
of the Tree-Leaves,
of Dreams & Premonitions
& of Nightfall
& Sunrise

God created from among the angels a group other than the recording angels. They are in charge of every seed in the earth and every leaf that falls to the ground, and everything in nature, both wet and dry, green and dead.

> *Not a leaf falleth but He knoweth it, not a grain amid the darkness of the earth, naught of wet or dry but it is noted in a clear record.*[68]

They also oversee the events of human and other beings that enter into the realm of uninhabited nature. If a human being is somewhere without help, he should say: "O invisible servants of God, support me with your help! And may God's mercy be with you." Ahmad ibn Hanbal said: "I went on pilgrimage five times, and on three of these five times I was on foot. Once I lost my way in the desert, so I kept repeating: 'O servants of God, guide me to the right way!' and I found my way not long after that." If one utters this prayer sincerely, the angels will guide him and protect him from the harms of travel and the hostility of rebel spirits.

The angels of nature fall under the authority of the Archangel Michael, and they have under them angelic legions and hosts constantly asking for forgiveness on behalf of human beings. Their intercession is according to the infinite numbers of the species and genera of nature they oversee. They ask intercession from the Lord and Creator of everything great and small. Even tree-leaves cause forgiveness of human beings, and the Lord of creation blesses human beings through them.

A famous saint had purified himself to the extent that he could hear the intercession of the angels of tree-leaves and of all nature, and he began to recite with them:

> *Praise be to the God of creation,*
> *The Lord of everything,*
> *Who created before the sky was hoisted*

---

68 Surat al-An'am, 6:59

*and the earth flattened,*
*Before the mountains were erected*
*and the springs made to burst forth,*
*Before the oceans were contained and the rivers tamed,*
*Before the sun was set alight and the moon and the stars,*
*Who wrote in the Book of His knowledge the name*
*Of every single rain-drop, of every leaf and seed,*
*Who owns whatever descends from the sky*
*And ascends from the earth,*
*And whatever grows under it,*
*And has entrusted it to His servants,*
*The loyal, unwavering, tireless angels.*

He also created the angel of dreams and premonitions. A Tradition of Prophet Muhammad says, "The good dream is one forthysixth part of prophecy." Specific angels that display visions and sounds to the sleeper. These pictures take a physical shape that can be sensed within the dream of individuals. Every dream fits the dreamer. This is proven by the fact that a sleeper in a place where there are many non-sleepers, sees what no-one else sees at the same time. That is because each person has his or her own individual angel in charge of sending the information contained in their dreams.

Thus dreams may be real, confirming what might happen in the future of that individual, except that he is seeing it happen beforehand. On the other hand, the dream may refer to a specific item of knowledge, phenomenal or spiritual, concerning the dreamer in his daily life. In either case it may be good tidings or a warning.

Abu Bakr Bin Furq was writing on the subject of dreams that warn us about a future event and their relation to the angelic realm. He fell asleep one Tuesday night in the year 1165. He saw an angel approach him clad in a beautiful, subtle body of light. The angel said to him: "God has created us and He has created you. It is He Who causes you to live and to die; He Who resurrects you and brings you to Paradise; He Who connects you with your soul after death. Everything that we receive in heaven is from him, and everything that

you receive on earth is from Him." The angel disappeared and the sleeper woke up. He wrote: "I knew at once that the angel had provided me with all the knowledge I needed to complete my work. When I finished writing, my book on angels and dreams numbered six hundred pages."

God created an angel named Sharahil who is the master manager of night-time. When the time for night is due every evening, he dangles a black diamond from the Western horizon, and when the sun sees that diamond it moves to its goal even faster, for it is under order not to set until it has seen that diamond. That is why the sun always seems to set faster when it is nearer nightfall. At dawn, another angel named Harahil who is entrusted with sunrise, brings with him a white diamond and dangles it over the Eastern horizon. Like the poles of some giant magnet, these angelic diamonds act to maintain the rotation of the earth and ensure the orderly progression of the night and day.

The sun cannot rise before seeing it. When it sees that diamond it is ordered to rise. The sun never rises willingly, but is pushed and goaded by seventy thousand angels every time.

These angels address the sun in very severe terms, saying: "Will you rise, or shall we beat you and stone you?"

But the sun answers: "How can I rise when I know that I shall be worshipped instead of the Creator?"

The angels continue: "The Lord orders you to rise, so rise!"

This takes place continuously, as the sun is always rising somewhere, and the angels sometimes have to make true their threats. That is why the sun is "stoned" with asteroids that fall into it, causing huge deflagrations and forming enormous craters. When it finally rises, seven other angels are in charge of dumping snow onto it, without which everything on earth would burn.

*It is not for the sun to overtake the moon, nor does the night outstrip the day. They float each in an orbit (lawfully ordained).*[69]

*By the sun and his brightness,*
*And the moon when she followeth him,*
*And the day when it enshroudeth him,*
*And the heaven and Him who built it,*
*And the earth and Him who spread it,*
*And a soul and Him who perfected it,*
*And inspired it with conscience of what is wrong for it and what is right!*
*He is indeed successful who causeth it to grow,*
*And he is indeed a failure who stunteth it......*[70]

The sun never rises willingly, but is pushed and goaded by seventy thousand angels every time. These angels address the sun in very severe terms, saying:

"Will you rise, or shall we beat you and stone you?"

But the sun answers: "How can I rise when I know that I shall be worshipped instead of the Creator?"

The angels continue: "The Lord orders you to rise, so rise!"

This takes place continuously, as the sun is always rising somewhere, and the angels sometimes have to make true their threats. That is why the sun is "stoned" with asteroids that fall into it, causing huge deflagrations and forming enormous craters. When it finally rises, seven other angels are in charge of dumping snow onto it, without which everything on earth would burn.

---

[69] Surah Yasin, 36:40

[70] Surat al-Layl, 91:1-10

Angels,
a Saint
and Speaking
in Tongues

The Prophet Muhammad showed his companions the unlimited worship of creation by allowing them to hear the praise to God of stones, animals, and trees. All of creation constantly praises God and makes prostration to Him.

> *And unto God maketh prostration whatsoever is in the heavens and whatsoever is in the earth of living creatures, and the angels also, and they are not proud.*[71]

Human beings are raised to a most honorable level by being listed the angels. That is why the angels shower special blessings on human beings who remember their Creator, and God boasts to his angels about them with the words: "Look at My servants who leave their pleasures despite themselves in order to worship Me."

> *Lo! Those who say: our Lord is God, and afterwards are upright, the angels descend upon them, saying: fear not nor grieve, but hear good tidings of the paradise which ye are promised.*[72]

The Prophet said that God created special angels who roam the earth to find people engaged in His *dhikr* (Remembrance). When the angels find such a group reciting His praises and chanting His names, they call each other and encompass that group in layer upon layer of angels until they reach the nearest heaven, the distance of which is in God's knowledge. Then God asks His angels: "What are my servants doing?" He asks not because He does not know, but because He wants the answer to be spoken outloud for us to know it.

The angels answer: "They are praising You and magnifying Your name, and glorifying You, and reciting Your beautiful Attributes!"

God then asks: "Have My servants seen Me?" When the angels answer: "No,"

---

71 Surat an-Nahl, 16:49

72 Surat al-Fussilat, 41:30

God asks: "What kind of praise would they make if they actually see Me?"

The angels answer: "O our Lord! If they see you, they are not going to be able to stop worshipping You, praising You, and declaring their love for You."

God then asks: "What are My servants asking?" The angels reply: "They are asking for Your Paradise."

God asks: "Did they see it?" The angels reply: "O our Lord! No, they did not see it."

"What if they see it?" God asks.

The angels reply: "If they were to see it they would be even more attracted to it, to the point of forgetting everything else in their lives!"

God then asks: "What are they running from?"

The angels answer: "They are running away from hellfire, which they fear greatly."

"Have they seen it?" God asks.

"O our Lord! No, they have not seen it," the angels reply.

"What if they see it, what then?" God asks.

The angels answer: "If they see your fire, they are going to be more intent on fleeing from it, to the point of forgetting everything else in their lives!" At that time God says: "O My angels in heaven and on earth! I am taking you as witnesses of My word that I have forgiven them." One of the angels says: "O my Lord! there was someone among them who does not belong to their group, but came

to them for some other need." God says: "If one were only to sit in the company of such a group, his sins also will be forgiven, and he has nothing to fear."

God's speech to the angels and their replies form a heart-melting dialogue that encourages and uplifts the hearts of believers. God is telling us to come together and love and help each other, and forgive each other, all for the sake of the fact that He created us and He loves us. The greatest kind of gathering, however, is the gathering where nothing other than God is mentioned or remembered among those gathered. Even to sit near such a gathering though not participating in it, insures one's forgiveness in God's divine presence. God mentions us in an exalted assembly and a gathering far better than ours when we mention him.

The following is what happened to one of the saints during his last sickness. He said: "O God! I felt afraid of you before, but today I am beseeching You: You know that I did not love this world more than You. I did not try to cheat and deceive, to hoard palaces and farms and properties full of fruitful trees, and cattle, and wells. But you know that all the time I tried to help the poor, visit the sick, help those who asked, welcome strangers, and care for your creation. You know that I was running to the angelic gatherings of good people, chanting and singing and calling on You. You know that I was seeking the help of Your angels. O God! You know that my heart longs for You. O my Lord! that pain of love in me takes away my mind and causes me to faint, and I cannot carry it anymore." At that point he fainted. When he woke up he continued: "O God! You know that I have a son who died as a martyr, and he just told me in his angelic form that he had been in a gathering of angels, prophets, truthful saints, martyrs, and righteous people. O God! let me be in a similar gathering also." At that time the angels surrounded him and became visible to him, greeting him and smiling upon him and encouraging him with kind words. He was seen rising in the air and calling out the names of the angels. He began to say: "That is Artiya'il, and that is Hara'il, and this is the angel of shadows, and that is the angel of the wind, and this is the angel of the unborn, and that

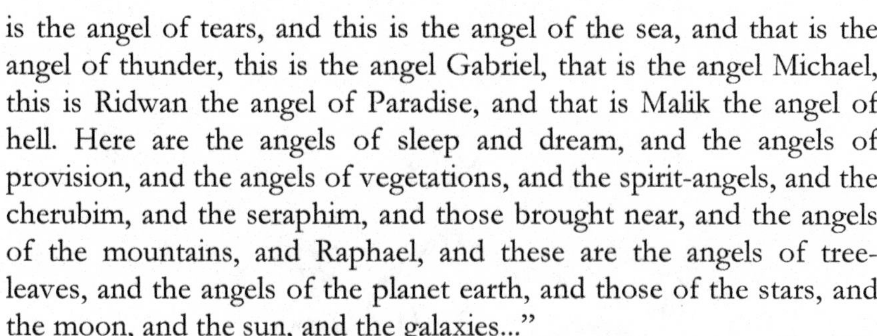

is the angel of tears, and this is the angel of the sea, and that is the angel of thunder, this is the angel Gabriel, that is the angel Michael, this is Ridwan the angel of Paradise, and that is Malik the angel of hell. Here are the angels of sleep and dream, and the angels of provision, and the angels of vegetations, and the spirit-angels, and the cherubim, and the seraphim, and those brought near, and the angels of the mountains, and Raphael, and these are the angels of tree-leaves, and the angels of the planet earth, and those of the stars, and the moon, and the sun, and the galaxies..."

Then the saint began to speak in a language that no-one could understand, until he finally asked the angel of death to take his soul in order to reach his Creator and be placed there as an angelic power. He died with open eyes suffused with light. "

God's speech to the angels and their replies form a heart-melting dialogue that encourages and uplifts the hearts of believers. God is telling us to come together and love and help each other, and forgive each other, all for the sake of the fact that He created us and He loves us. The greatest kind of gathering, however, is the gathering where nothing other than God is mentioned or remembered among those gathered. Even to sit near such a gathering though not participating in it, insures one's forgiveness in God's divine presence. God mentions us in an exalted assembly and a gathering far better than ours when we mention him.

PART THREE
-THE FUTURE

# Israfil, Archangel of the Trumpet Blast

*The Supreme Horror will not grieve them, and the angels will welcome them, saying: This is your Day which ye were promised.*[73]

*A day when the heavens with the clouds will be rent asunder and the angels will be sent down, a great descent.*[74]

*Then how will it be with them when the angels gather them, smiting their faces and their backs?*[75]

After God created the Throne He created the Trumpet (*sur*) and hung it on the Throne. Then He said: "Be!" and the angel Israfil was. He ordered him to take up the Trumpet which is like a white pearl and transparent like glass. He made holes in the Trumpet according to the number of every spirit and angel created in creation without duplication. In the middle of the Trumpet there is an opening bigger than the sky and the earth put together. Israfil is able to stop that opening from top to bottom by placing his mouth over it. The length of this Trumpet is seventy thousand light-years and its body is divided into seven trunks.

God said to Israfil: "I order you to blow this Trumpet when I shall tell you." Israfil stands at the base of the Throne and awaits God's order. He is so near to God that between him and his Lord there are only seven veils of light. One of his wings is in the East, another in the West, one encompasses the seven earths, and the fourth wing is on his head to protect his eyes from the light of God.

One day the Prophet was sitting with Gabriel, and the sky opened. Gabriel humbled himself and appeared to fall to the ground as if prostrating, and an immense angel dressed in white appeared before the Prophet and said: "O Muhammad! God sends you greetings and salutations and gives you the choice between being an angel-prophet or a servant-prophet." The Prophet answered: "The

---

73 Surat al-Anbiya, 21:103

74 Surat al-Furqan, 25:25

75 Surah Muhammad, 47:27

happiest time of my life is when my Lord calls me: 'O My servant!' O servant of God! I choose to be a servant-prophet." And Gabriel revealed:

*God chooseth from the angels messengers, and also from mankind. Lo! God is Hearer, Seer.*[76]

Then the angel disappeared. The Prophet asked Gabriel: "Who was that angel?" Gabriel said: "That was Israfil. Since the day God created him, he has not raised his eyes from the ground for fear of his Lord. Between him and God there are seven veils of light and if he were to pass only one of them he would be annihilated. The Preserved Tablet whereupon the destinies of mankind are written lies before him. Whenever God allows for something to exist in heaven or on earth that Tablet is raised up and he reads it. If a task falls within the sphere of the Angel of Death, He orders him to perform it. If in my sphere He orders me to do it, and if in Michael's sphere He orders him in the same manner. I did not think that Israfil would come down to earth before the Day of Judgment and that is why I was afraid!"

On the Day of Judgment God will order Israfil to blow that Trumpet. Upon the first sounding of the Trumpet all bad things are lifted and taken away from the earth. Wrongdoings and all that is related to it will disappear. The heavenly books will shine in every place. Angels will appear and reveal the places where they have been kept in their pristine state. The memory of heavenly teachings will become fresh again in people's minds. All manner of good character, dignity, honor, mercy, and blessings will be brought over all the earth and become the norm. Angels will feel welcome to walk upon the earth for the first time. No-one will have power to do any harm in the world. Belief in God and knowledge of spiritual things will become the daily conversation of everyone young and old. Angelic light will increase upon the earth to such a degree that everything sad

76 Surat al-Hajj, 22:75

will become happy, everything bad will become good, everything poor will become rich, and everything ugly will become beautiful.

Upon the second sounding of the trumpet, all beings in the heavens and on earth will enter a state of perplexity and become afraid. They will fall down on their faces and faint believing the Day of Judgment has dawned upon them. This is described in the Quran,

> *And the trumpet is blown , and all who are in the heavens and on the earth swoon away, save him whom God willeth. Then it is blown a second time, and behold them standing waiting!*[77]

The sound of that trumpet will be so awesome and terrifying that all beings will lose consciousness. The earth will begin to roll and heave, the stars will fall from the heavens, the light will disappear, the sun and the moon will lose their light, and all will be plunged into abysmal darkness. The mountains will jump from their places and turn to dust, and rise as clouds over the earth. The water of the oceans will dry up. Just as wind carries away chaff, so creation will be blown away by those cataclysmic storms.

The good people will be covered with garments of light and mercy which the angels will bring down in waves. The angels will smite all wrongdoings and shameful actions and they will disappear like dust that must be removed from furnishings in a huge palace. They will bring light and smile on those who believed in them like parents smile on their children, as reassurance on that day. For on Judgment Day there is no-one who will not need the support of reassurance.

Upon the third sounding of the Trumpet God will dress and adorn all human beings with angelic power and send them into the throng of His servants. There they will inhabit that divine indescribable light that enables them to reach the everlasting life of Paradise.

---

[77] Surat az-Zumar, 39:68

# Angels of Mercy and Wrath

*Lo! As for those whom the angels take in death while they wrong themselves, the angels will ask: In what were ye engaged? They will say: We were oppressed in the land. The angels will say: Was not God's earth spacious that ye could have migrated therein? As for such, their habitation will be hell, an evil journey's end.*[78]

*If thou couldst see how the angels receive those who disbelieve, smiting their faces and their backs and saying: Taste the punishment of burning!*[79]

*Those who have been given knowledge will say: Disgrace this day and evil upon the disbelievers, whom the angels cause to die while they are wronging themselves.*[80]

*Those whom the angels cause to die when they are good. They say: Peace be unto you! Enter the Garden because of what ye used to do.*[81]

*O ye who believe! Ward off from yourselves and your families a fire whereof the fuel is men and stones, over which are set angels, strong, severe, who resist not God in that which He commanded them, but do that which they are commanded.*[82]

*We have appointed only angels to be wardens of the fire, and their number have We made to be a stumbling-block for those who disbelieve.*[83]

---

78 Surat an-Nisa, 4:97

79 Surat al-Anfal, 8:50

80 Surat an-Nahl, 16:27-28

81 Surat an-Nahl, 16:32

82 Surat at-Tahrim, 66:6

83 Surat al-Mudaththir, 74:31

Both the angels of mercy and wrath question the dying about how they spent their life. People answer them: "We were weak and oppressed by tyrants who deceived us, and that is why we could not follow the truth although we knew it." But angels will ask them: "Why did you not migrate to other lands were you would have been free from tyranny? Our decision is that you will be called to account for what you did."

Another meaning is that angels are messengers of God, and God is the creator of love and mercy. God created these angels from the light of His attribute: "al-Rahman," the Merciful. They are green, the color of nature, trees, and gardens; for sight of green brings tranquility and peace to the heart. When angels question people it means that they are seeking excuses to exonerate them.

A divine messenger knows how things stand in reality. He is aware that these people committed sins. He knows also that the decision has already been taken concerning them. In the first place, we should know, it is unnecessary for the angels to ask them any questions. The questioning only enables human beings to be excused because they are "weak and oppressed." Thus the first words of their plea in 4:97, "weak and oppressed," are like a lawyer's opening statement which ends up with God's pardon.

In reality these angels are advocates of peace between the servant and His Lord. They are charged with bringing out of the servant's mouth the excuse that God will accept to blot out his sin. That is why God states in the very next verses:

> *Except those who are really weak and oppressed, men, women, and children who have no means in their power nor can they find a way to escape-- for these there is hope that God will forgive, for God doth blot out sins and forgive again and again.*[84]

[84] Surat an-Nisa, 4:98-99

The severity of the wardens of hell is proportionate to the distance of a soul from the sight of God in the hereafter. The great saint Bayazid al-Bistami said: "There are slaves who, if they were veiled from the sight of God in Paradise, would beg to be taken out of it the way the inhabitants of the Fire beg to be taken out of it." This is because once the heart has been purified and the human soul is taken out and brought to the angelic world, it cannot be satisfied by anything less than what the angels themselves enjoy, which is the sight of God. Sight of God at the exclusion of everything else including Paradise and hell is the meaning of true worship according to the verse:

> *I did not create jinn and humankind except to worship Me.*[85]

Concerning this delicate topic the saint Nasir al-Din said:

*When God created hell, He created it*
*In perfect tenderness and mercy.*
*Wait until the beauty of 'the Merciful, the Compassionate'*
*Comes out from the pavilion of inaccessibility*
*And tells you without tongue nor human speech*
*What mystery is hidden in the saying:*
*'A time will come when watercress will grow*
*From the deepest pit of hell!'*

[85] Surat adh-Dhariyat, 51:56

# Gabriel, the Archangel Servant

*And if ye aid one another against him (Muhammad), then lo! God, even He, is his protecting Friend, and Gabriel and the righteous among the believers; and furthermore the angels are his helpers.*[86]

*Who is an enemy to God, and His angels, and His Messengers, and Gabriel, and Michael! Then, lo! God Himself is an enemy to the disbelievers.*[87]

When God created the Archangel Gabriel, He made him tall and adorned with a celestial white dress sown with red rubies and pearls. His complexion is white as snow. He has one thousand six hundred wings. The distance between every two wings is five hundred years. He has a long neck, feet of red and green diamond, and yellow legs. He is covered with seventy thousand feathers of saffron from his head to his feet. On each feather there is one moon and many stars. Between his two eyes there is a sun. God created him five hundred years after He created Michael. Every night he bathes in a river in Paradise. When he emerges from the river he shakes off the water. Out of seventy thousand drops that come from him God creates from every drop an angel that circumambulates God's House in Paradise until Judgment Day.

Before dawn, Gabriel immerses himself again in one of the rivers that flow at the right of the Throne. He is then covered with light upon light, beauty upon beauty, and majesty upon majesty. He emerges and shakes himself off and out of every drop that comes from his feathers God creates seventy thousand angels whom He sends to earth, never to come back until Judgment Day. They are to take care of people, to guard them, help them, entertain them, and appear to them in all kinds of forms. Then Gabriel stands before God and his legs tremble continuously. From each tremor God creates one hundred thousand angels who do not speak except by God's permission. If permission is granted to them their only words

---

86 Surat at-Tahrim, 66:4

87 Surat al-Baqara, 2:98

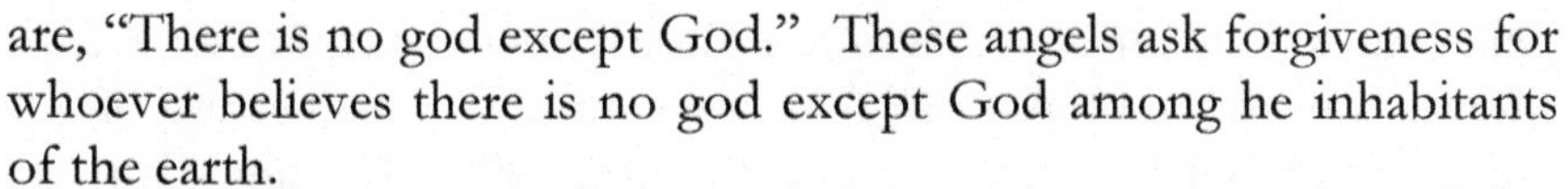


are, "There is no god except God." These angels ask forgiveness for whoever believes there is no god except God among he inhabitants of the earth.

God has inspired Gabriel to stand at the door of servanthood, to acknowledge the dignity of Lordship, to pay in the field of gratefulness to God and to know His majestic power: "I have granted you much," said God to him, "so listen to what is revealed to you. You are My messenger to My prophets and you are My flag of guidance."

Gabriel's name in the divine presence is the Servant of God (Abd Allah). He is known by that name among the angels. He is always seen wearing a green cloak that fills up the space between heaven and earth. Gabriel appeared to Prophet Muhammad many times in the shape of different human beings. One day Prophet Muhammad asked to see Gabriel in his original form. Gabriel told him to meet him at a certain place at night. When the Prophet came to the appointed spot he saw Gabriel standing in the sky with his wings outstretched, until there was no more heaven nor horizon in sight. He covered the entire sky all around the firmament. Prophet Muhammad's uncle Hamza asked also to see Gabriel in his original form and Prophet Muhammad told him, "You cannot." When he insisted, Prophet Muhammad told him to sit down on a bench near the Kabah. Then he told him to raise his eyes and look. When he raised his eyes a little bit he began to see feet of green emerald and he instantly fainted. Gabriel disappeared.

Gabriel is one of the foremost among those brought near to God. Whenever God mentions a servant that is chanting and calling his Lord, He tells Gabriel, "Praise that person because he is praising Me." Gabriel then makes all the inhabitants of heaven praise that person.

God has given Gabriel the responsibility to look after the needs of His servants on earth. He says to him, "O Gabriel! Take care of the heart of My believer. Remove from the heart of My

believing servant the sweetness that he experienced in My love. Let Me see how he will long for Me and whether his love is true." Then He says, "O Gabriel! Put back into the heart of My servant what you have taken from him because he is trustworthy. I am giving him more."

One day Gabriel came to Prophet Muhammad crying. When Prophet Muhammad asked him why he was crying, he replied, "And why not cry? I swear by God that never since He created hell have my eyes stopped crying for fear that I might make a mistake and He would put me there."

And he said, "God has told this world, 'O world! Be hard and difficult on those who love Me. Be a prison for them so that they will be eager to meet with Me and long for paradise as a deliverance."

Gabriel never came to a prophet except with four other angels. He said, "God has created a kingdom in this universe whose inhabitants ride the best piebald horses. Each of them carries a box containing a heavenly treasure. The life-span of each inhabitant as well as each horse is one thousand years. You can see neither their beginning nor their end." He was asked, "Who are these?" He replied, "Haven't you heard God's saying, 'No one knows His soldiers except He?' I see them in my ascending and my descending; I don't know where they come from or where they go. Their kingdom consists in seventy planets of gold, seventy planets of camphor and seventy planets of amber. Behind these planets are seventy thousand others. On each planet there is an infinite number of angels who know nothing about Adam and his children. They are kept for a completely different divine service. They never saw a creature who disobeyed God. They await God's order concerning the treasure that they are holding and do not use it for themselves."

After almost everyone dies on this planet God asks the angel of death to take all the remaining souls of every single created being, then asks him: "Who is left?"

The angel of death answers, "O My exalted Lord! There is only Michael, Gabriel, and myself left."

God says, "Take the soul of Michael." Then He asks, "Who is left?"

The angel of death says, "O my Lord, only Gabriel and myself are left."

Then God says, "Die, O angel of death." Then God turns to Gabriel and asks, "Who is left, O Gabriel?"

Gabriel answers, "Only Your Face remains, O my Lord, and Gabriel who is dead and extinguished." God then says to him, "You have to die." And immediately Gabriel falls down in prostration, shakes his wings, and dies.

Then God says, "I have created creation and I am the one to bring it back." Gabriel will be the second angel to be brought back to life after Israfil who blows the trumpet of Resurrection. He will be responsible for the scales of the deeds of human beings on the Day of Judgment.

# Angels and Material Energy

*Why bringest thou not angels unto us, if thou art of the truthful? We send not down the angels save with the Fact, and in that case the disbelievers would not be tolerated.*[88]

*"(We will not put faith in thee till) Thou cause the heaven to fall upon us piecemeal, as thou hast pretended, or bring God and the angels as a warrant."*[89]

*And those who look not for a meeting with Us say: Why are angels not sent down unto us and why do we not see our Lord? Assuredly they think too highly of themselves and are scornful with great pride. On the day when they behold the angels, on that day there will be no good tidings for the guilty; and they will cry: A forbidding ban!*[90]

The unbelievers refuse to believe in God, His angels, and His revelations. They only believe in material things. To them, belief in what one sees and the material is more practical. Such practical-minded people are blind to the reality for which God has given children, prophets, saints, and believers eyes and power to see. To those the power is given to feel and to see the angelic beings that reside among us and to visualize these spiritual things. When we see such matters with believing eyes, we become receivers clearly catching the images sent by the spiritual emissaries. We visualize them as real, not false, pictures in our daily lives.

Energy is a form of angelic power. Human beings have been granted the permission to use it. As we can develop the instruments to use these energies with greater sophistication, we can achieve more and more visible powers in the material world. The energy that is used to light a lamp, convey sound to a loudspeaker, see images on a television, run a car, launch a satellite, keep us warm in winter and cool in summer, is all the same. Only the instruments change.

---

[88] Surat al-Hijr, 15:7-8

[89] Surat an-Najm, 17:92

[90] Surat al-Furqan, 25:21-22

Similarly, angelic energy changes from one person to another. The source is one and the same. When human beings elevate themselves to higher states of purity, they can use this energy to be more powerful and visible to others as servants of God, and they themselves become messengers of this angelic power.

Angels and their power are not sent down to satisfy the whim or curiosity of unbelievers. They are sent to bring inspiration to God's servants, to execute His decrees, to help people in their daily lives and resolve their problems. They raise and protect children through their childhood in order to bring all human beings to the highest level they can reach in the divine presence. Angels and their angelic powers do not help tyrants and oppressors dominate this world. Instead, they look for soft-hearted people to direct them and instruct them on how to keep this world orderly and pure from spiritual and material pollutions. They disconnect their energies from anyone who tries to harm nature, animals, or human beings, or exploit them for selfish purposes.

The angelic source of power rests on three hundred and sixty pillars. Each pillar can contain the entire visible universe. The distance between one pillar and the next is five hundred thousand of God's years:

*One day in the sight of God is like one thousand of your years"*[91]

God has created for this angelic power one million six hundred thousand heads. Each head has one million six hundred thousand faces. Each face is bigger than this universe by one million six hundred thousand times, and each face has one million six hundred thousand mouths. Each mouth contains one million six hundred thousand tongues. Each tongue praises God with one million six hundred thousand different languages. For each praise, God creates one million six hundred thousand angels. All these

[91] Surat as-Sajdah, 32:5.

angels shall say on the Judgment Day: "O God! give the reward of our praises to Your believing servants among human beings."

# Archangel 'Azra'il and the Other Angels of Death

*If thou couldst see, when the wrong-doers reach the pangs of death and the angels stretch their hands out, saying: Deliver up your souls!"*[92]

*Say: "The Angel of Death, who hath charge concerning you, will gather you and afterward unto your Lord ye will be returned."*[93]

In these verses the Angel of Death and his assistants are sent to take the soul of those destined to die. Who is the Angel of Death? When God wanted to create Adam, he sent one of the Angels of the Throne to bring some of the earth's clay to fashion Adam from it. When the angel came to earth to take the clay, the earth told him: "I beseech you by the One Who sent you not to take anything from me to make someone who will be punished one day." When the angel returned empty-handed, God asked him why he did not bring back any clay.

The angel said: "The earth beseeched me by Your greatness not to take anything from it." Then God sent another angel, but the same thing happened, and then another, until God decided to send ʿAzra'il, the Angel of Death. The earth spoke to him as it had spoken to the others, but ʿAzra'il said: "Obedience to God is better than obedience to you, even if you beseech me by His greatness." And ʿAzra'il took clay from the earth's east and its west, its north and its south, and brought it back to God. God poured some water of paradise on this clay and it became soft, and from it He created Adam.

---

[92] Surat al-Anʿam, 6:93

[93] Surat as-Sajdah, 32:11

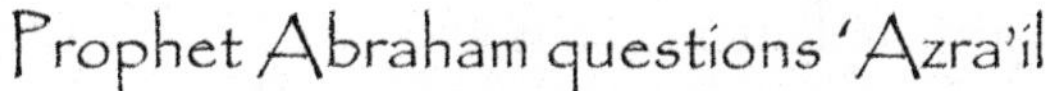



## Prophet Abraham questions ʿAzra'il

The Prophet Abraham once asked ʿAzra'il who has two eyes in the front of his head and two eyes in the back: "O Angel of Death! What do you do if one man dies in the east and another in the west, or if a land is stricken by the plague, or if two armies meet in the field?" The angel said: "O Messenger of God! the names of these people are inscribed on the *Lawh al-Mahfuz*: It is the 'Preserved Tablet' on which all human destinies are engraved. I gaze at it incessantly. It informs me of the moment when the lifetime of any living being on earth has come to an end, be it one of mankind or one of the beasts. There is also a tree next to me, called the Tree of Life. It is covered with myriads of tiny leaves, smaller than the leaves of the olive-tree and much more numerous. Whenever a person is born on earth, the tree sprouts a new leaf, and on this leaf is written the name of that person. It is by means of this tree that I know who is born and who is to die. When a person is going to die, his leaf begins to wilt and dry, and it falls from the tree onto the tablet. Then this person's name is erased from the Preserved Tablet. This event happens forty days before the actual death of that person. We are informed forty days in advance of his impending death. That person himself may not know it and may continue his life on earth full of hope and plans. However, we here in the heavens know and have that information. That is why God has said:

> *Your sustenance has been written in the heavens and decreed for you,*[94]

and it includes the life-span. The moment we see in heaven that leaf wilting and dying we mix it into that person's provision, and from the fortieth day before his death he begins to consume his leaf from the Tree of Life without knowing it. Only forty days then remain of his life in this world, and after that there is no provision for him in it. Then I summon the spirits by God's leave, until they are present

[94] Surat adh-Dhariyat, 51:22

right before me, and the earth is flattened out and left like a dish before me, from which I partake as I wish, by God's order."

## Two Deaths

A certain king once went on a trip to one of his provinces. He set out on his journey, dressed in a sumptuous array and puffed up with pride. A man poorly dressed approached and greeted him from the side of the road; but the king would not answer. The man caught the bridles of the king's horse and none of the king's soldiers could make him let go. The king cried: "Let go of the bridle!" The man said: "First grant me my request." The king said: "Release the bridle and I promise to hear your request." The man said: "No, you must hear it right away," and he pulled harder on the reins. The king said: "What is your request?" The man replied: "Let me whisper it in your ear, for it is a secret." The king leaned down and the man whispered to him: "I am the Angel of Death." The king's face became pale and he stammered: "Let me go home and bid farewell to my family, and wrap up my affairs." But ʿAzra'il said: "By the One Who sent me, you will never see your family and your wealth in this world again!" He took his soul there and then, and the king fell from his horse like a wooden log.

The Angel of Death went on his way and saw a believer walking by himself on the road. The angel greeted him, and he gave back his greeting. The angel said: "I have a message for you." "Yes, my brother, what is it?" "I am the Angel of Death." The believer's face brightened with a big smile. "Welcome, welcome!" He said. "As God is my witness, I was waiting for you more impatiently than for anyone else." "O my brother!" the Angel of Death said, "perhaps you have a matter that you wish to settle first, so go and take care of it, for there is no rush." "As God is my witness," the believer said: "there is nothing I wish more dearly than to meet my Lord." The angel said: "Choose the way in which you would like me to take your soul, for so I have been ordered to ask you." The believer said:

"Then let me pray two cycles of prayer, and take my soul while I am kneeling in prostration."

## 'Azra'il Takes the Life of an Ascetic

One day, the master of ascetics, Ibrahim ibn Adham, was by the sea-shore on a snowy day. Heavy, dark clouds were filling the sky and he was shivering with cold. He made his prayers on a plank of wood and sat in meditation all night. In the early morning he took a shower and made a small hut out of the wood to shelter him from the weather. He resumed his meditation and thanked God for his life. At that moment, God said to the Angel of Death: "My servant Ibrahim's fervent love for Me has become unbearable upon him, therefore go down and take his soul and let him enter My paradise." The Angel of Death thought that Ibrahim ibn Adham would be like others, unwilling to give up his soul and putting up resistance. He veiled himself with seven veils so that he would not be recognized, and he appeared to Ibrahim as a very old man. He said to him: "O my brother! can you share your shelter with me?" Ibrahim replied: "It is not necessary to share it, I will give it to you, because I was expecting you since last night to come and take me to my Lord." The angel of death was very surprised and asked him: "How did you recognize me despite my veils?" Ibrahim replied: "When God ordered you to take my soul, I was present there with you. Take me and let me be in the presence of my Beloved."

## The Death of a Subject of King Solomon

One day, the Angel of Death entered King Solomon's presence and looked at one of Solomon's subjects in a fierce way, then left. The man asked Solomon: "Who was that?" He said: "That was the Angel of Death." The man said: "I saw him looking at me as if he wanted my soul!" Solomon said: "What do you want me to do?" He said: "I want you to order the winds to take me and carry me to India so that I will be safe." Solomon summoned the angel of the

winds, who appeared in front of him with his 660 wings. He carried all winds within his wings. He put the man inside one of his wings and took him to India. The Angel of Death then came to Solomon again and Solomon said to him: "I saw you looking at one of my people." "Yes," replied the angel, "I was surprised to see him here with you, because I was ordered to take his soul from a place in India!"

## Dede Korkut

Dede Korkut was the bravest warrior of his time. His exploits reached a point where he considered himself invincible in the land, and challenged all creation to defeat him and his brave young men in combat. God heard his words and was displeased with his pride. So he sent him the Angel of Death to take his soul. ʿAzra'il came to him as he was feasting in his palace and stood before him without saying a word. Dede Korkut said: "I did not see you come in; who are you?" The angel replied: "I am not one to ask permission from the likes of you, and I came to teach you a lesson." The young man immediately rose to his feet and ordered that the visitor be caught, but he changed himself into a bird and flew out through the chimney.

Dede Korkut ordered his horse saddled and everyone rushed in hot pursuit of the strange bird. Soon he found himself lost in the middle of the forest, and the angel suddenly appeared again in front of him. "I got you now!" exclaimed Dede Korkut. "No," said the angel, "I got you," and he brought him down from his horse and stood on his chest, pinning him to the ground. Dede Korkut began to cry and said: "I feel weaker than I ever felt before. What did you do to me?" ʿAzra'il said: "I am the angel of death, so prepare yourself to leave this life." He replied: "I beseech you to give me more time and I apologize to you if my boasting offended you." ʿAzra'il said: "Do not apologize to me and do not beseech me. I am a creature like you, and I only follow orders from the Almighty." Dede Korkut said: "Then get out of my way, and stop wasting my time!" And he began to pray to God: "Forgive my boasting, O my God! and give me another chance, as I apologize for offending you. You are the Almighty over your creation."

God liked Dede's words and instructed ʿAzra'il to give him a respite. ʿAzra'il said: "God has decided to let you live on the condition that you find someone else to die in your place." Dede Korkut thought: "I will ask my father, he is old and will not refuse me." He went to him and told him his story, but he replied: "O my son! I slaved my lifelong in order to relish my old age. I am sorry, but I am not ready to die in your place." Dede Korkut thought: "Surely my mother will not refuse me." He went to her but she said: "O my son! I gave my life to you many times already, when I bore you, fed you, raised you and took care of you. Now the rest of my life belongs at your father's side, as company for his old age."

The young man was crestfallen and he went home, resigned to die. When his young wife saw his sadness, she asked what troubled him and he said: "O my beloved wife! the Angel of Death is about to come and take my life unless I find someone else willing to die in my place, and my own father and mother have refused me, so who can I find now?" His wife answered, "O my beloved husband! why didn't you ask me? I am happy to give you what even your father and mother cannot give you. Take my life so that yours can be spared." When Dede Korkut, the Fierce Warrior heard these words, his heart melted and tears came to his eyes. He turned to God and said: "O my Lord! forgive me, take my life and spare my wife, for she is worthier and braver than me." God was again pleased to hear those words, and he decided to spare both Dede Korkut and his wife. Instead, He sent ʿAzra'il to take the life of his parents as they had been blessed with a long and happy life.

God wrote on the palms of the Angel of Death in letters of light: "In the Name of God, Most Merciful, Most Beneficent." He ordered the angel, whenever he had to take the soul of a Knower of God, to show him those letters of light which cause the soul of the

Knower to come out of is body like an element attracted to a magnet, or like light returning to its source.

## The Passing of King David

The Prophet narrated that David never accepted anyone entering his house, and he always locked all his doors whenever he went out. One day he went out for a certain matter and when he came back, he found a man in his house, standing and waiting for him. David was surprised to see him and he asked him what he was doing there. The man replied: "I am the one who needs no permission to enter, who does not fear kings, and whom no-one can resist." David said: "Then you are the Angel of Death, so welcome to you with fond love, for I was eagerly waiting for the moment when I shall be with my Beloved." And the Angel of Death took David's soul.

# The Angels of the Grave

*And though We should send down the angels unto them, and the dead should speak unto them, and We should gather against them all things in array, they would not believe unless God so willed. Howbeit, most of them are ignorant.*[95]

In this verse, God shows that devils and unbelievers never accept angels and belief in God, even if God shows them all kinds of signs. God has created two angels to visit every person who enters the grave, whether believer or unbeliever. One angel is called Munkar, the other Nakir. They appear dressed in a blue light and big golden eyes with pupils of diamond that send quick lightning bolts. Their voice is loud like thunder, their teeth like emeralds, their fragrance that of roses. They have fine, long hair. They bring with them all kinds of treasures from heaven in one hand, and all kinds of punishments in the other. If that person is a believer, the angels open up his grave and make it seventy times larger in size, adorn it with their light, and turn it into a plot of Paradise filled with all sorts of pleasures until Judgment Day. If the person was an unbeliever, they will constrict his grave into a smaller and smaller place until he feels pressure upon his bones, and he is left in that position until Judgment Day.

It is related through Ali ibn Abi Talib that when Umar ibn al-Khattab died and the people buried him, the two angels of death Munkar and Nakir appeared to him carrying with them the garments and lights of paradise with which to dress him. They asked him: "Who is your Lord?" He replied: "Why are you asking me this question? Don't you know who is my Lord and yours?" They replied: "We have to ask you and you have to answer." Umar said: "I cannot raise my voice very much. Please approach so I can give you my answer." When Munkar and Nakir approached, Umar punched one angel in the eye, kicked the other, and shouted: "How dare you ask me who is my Lord? Do you think that I am forgetting my Lord when I just came to the grave from a short distance, and I was

---

95 Surat al-Anʿam, 6:111

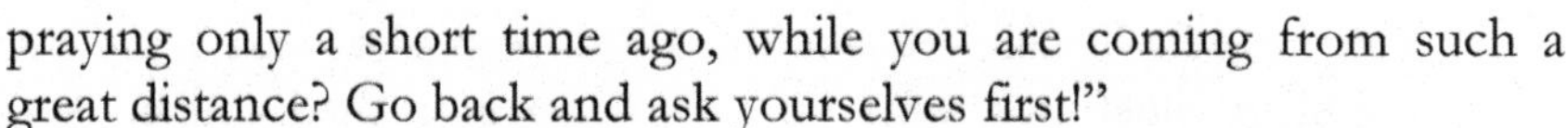


praying only a short time ago, while you are coming from such a great distance? Go back and ask yourselves first!"

When the great saint Abu Yazid died and they took him to the grave, some saw him in their dream, and he said: "The two angels came to interrogate me. When they asked me the question: 'Who is your Lord,' I answered: *'Tarihun bayna yadayh,'* 'I am lying helpless before Him!' Why do you ask me? But ask Him: Am I His servant? If he says to you: 'Yes,' then I have to be honored and lifted up to the highest stations in Paradise."

"The two angels said: 'This is strange discourse that makes one wonder. What does it mean?' I replied: 'Don't wonder so much at my words. I have more (to make you wonder more)! When God Almighty brought me forth from Adam's loins and asked him and all his descendants: 'Am I not your Lord?' I was of those who said: 'Yes! you are our Lord.' Where were you at that time? Were you present there?' The angels replied dumbfounded: 'No.' I continued: 'You were not present! Yet I still remember that day as if it were yesterday. Therefore, leave me alone and don't interfere between me and Him!'"

"One of the angels said to the other: 'This is Abu Yazid. He lived drunk with love of God, and he died drunk with the same love of God, and he was placed in his grave drunk with the love of God. When he is called on the Judgment Day, he will be drunk with the love of God.' Then they left me."

One time the Prophet Muhammad, peace be upon him, was attending the funeral of one of his Companions. On the way to bury him, the Prophet was walking on his toes in a very careful way, as if walking on eggs. They buried him, and they returned home. The Companions then asked the Prophet: "We saw something very strange today." The Prophet said: "I was astounded to see so many angels today, that there was no place to put my feet! The angels of God were filling every place, and they were surrounding that person to his last abode."

Many people can see and hear the angels of death, as the following story illustrates. One time, a rich person died and his son wanted to honor him in a special way. He advertised the following request in the city: “I will give whoever can stay in my father’s company in the grave for one night a sack of gold coins.” An old, very poor woodcutter who had a large family to feed said: “I will take that offer and it will help me to raise my children.” He followed the bier until they buried the man and left him behind in the grave, which was like a room with the coffin laid inside. That woodcutter prepared to spend the night in meditation.

At nightfall, as he sat silently, he began to hear voices speaking in different tongues, some familiar to him, some strange. He was terrified but he could not leave as the door was locked and he had to wait until morning. He took the rope which he used to carry wood, cut some part of it, and put it into his ears so as not to hear any voices. However, as much as he stopped his ears, he could not help but hear the voices more and more loudly. His heart sank within him, his feet and his entire body shook in fear at what he was hearing. Then he began to hear footsteps approaching him from behind.

As these footsteps drew closer, he realized that it was not one, but hundreds of men approaching. He closed his eyes in terror, afraid to see anything. He felt a touch on his shoulder and heard someone calling him by his name. He froze and wondered who it was that had entered this locked grave and was now calling him by name. He tried to open his eyes but he was unable because his fear was too great. Then he felt someone shaking him and he found himself opening his eyes and looking behind him. He saw an immense light filling the grave, as bright as the sun, and he saw two angels sitting on a throne, surrounded by hundreds of other angels who were carrying them to the dead body so that the questioning would begin. At that moment he remembered every single mistake, however minute, that he had done in his life. Yet he was relieved that the angels were coming not to ask him, but the dead man who lay next to him.

During that unpleasant scene, he heard the two angels saying to each other: "There is the dead person, and here is a live one. We have time to question the first one, but what about the other? He might leave, and it is better to begin with him, and ask the dead man later." He knew that there was no escaping from the hand of the angels and he surrendered to God's will. They said: "You! O So-and-So (calling him by his name), approach!" He loathed to approach them but he had no choice. They said: "We will not question you about what you did in the past but we will ask you about your present deeds. What are you carrying with you from the enjoyments of this earth?" They searched him, and found nothing other than an ax and a rope, the tools of a woodcutter. They said: "Tell us how you got these two pieces of material. How did you earn the money which you used to buy them? Did you get them by lawful means, by the sweat of your brow, or by some different ways?"

It took the man from evening to morning to answer to the angels' satisfaction on these two simple questions: How did he get the ax, and how did he get the rope? In the morning the man heard footsteps, and he realized that the dead man's son was coming to open the door of the grave. The woodcutter cried for deliverance, which he considered dearer and more precious than all of the pleasures of this life. He ran out as the dead man's son was telling him: "Take your money!" The woodcutter replied as he was running away: "For one ax and one rope they were questioning me until morning; if I take this sack of gold, they might question me forever! Keep the gold for yourself and the rich. I want to spend the rest of my life in love of God!"

The
Angels
Who Bring
Peace in the
Last Days

*Will they wait until God comes to them in canopies of clouds, with angels in His train and the question is thus settled?*[96]

In the last days, evil will be eradicated from the surface of the earth. Peace will be shining everywhere. It is related that at the end of times Jesus will reappear and descend upon the White Minaret at Damascus, both his hands resting upon the shoulders of two angels. He will be wearing two garments lightly dyes with saffron. He will be welcomes by a descendant of the prophet Muhammad who will be waiting for him with forty thousand angels, together with the believers who wil be waiting for a divine rescue. They will pray together and ask God to open for them a support to destroy tyranny and oppression, and to spread peace and love and happiness. God sent the angel Gabriel who related the message to Jesus, son of Mary, and to Mehdi, the grandson of the Prophet. The message will be: "God gave you the permission to use divine light for uplifting all humanity towards heaven and overcoming evil and oppression. They will then meet the Anti-Christ and his armies at the Lat gate near Jerusalem. A series of great battles will ensue at the end of which Jesus will kill the Anti-Christ, who is the enemy of good. God will then make Jesus the son of Mary, and Mehdi the descendant of the Prophet, the rulers of the world in the peace that follows the Great War at the end of times. Jesus will marry at that time, raise children, die, and be buried in Madina near the Prophet Muhammad, in the space left vacant for him there. Peace be upon them and upon the angels!

*Do not think that I have forgotten you, O angels!*
*Verily, even though the gulf is great between us,*
*I still love you, and my letters to you will never stop.*
*My love for you will never change.*
*My emotions are like a spring falling into your oceans.*
*I have left the distractions of my self to turn to you.*
*Your world has taken over mine, and shines over it.*
*I shall praise our Lord with your words, not mine,*

---

96 Surat al-Baqara, 2:10

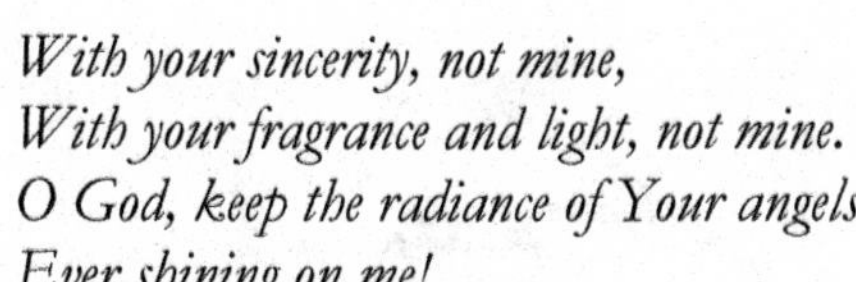

*With your sincerity, not mine,*
*With your fragrance and light, not mine.*
*O God, keep the radiance of Your angels*
*Ever shining on me!*

# Conclusion

*Lord of the heavens and the earth and all that is between them, the Beneficent; with Whom none can converse. On the day when the angels and the Spirit stand arrayed, they speak not, saving him whom the Beneficent alloweth and who speaketh right.*[97]

God shows in these words that the angels are from among His greatest creations. They stand second to him and they are His messengers of revelation sent to His prophets. He has honored them by letting them reveal the astounding knowledge in two ways: spiritually and phenomenally. He reveals it spiritually by letting prophets bring such knowledge in heavenly books and thereby guide others to the faith and honorable manners characteristic of the servants of God. He reveals it phenomenally by inspiring the hearts of humankind to investigate and discover the visible world and accumulate empirical data. Hence, they achieve the most sophisticated technology that can possibly be reached by them in every given century.

This opens another window into understanding the role of angels among human beings. Scientists are actually using the energies that radiate from the angels on this earth to build up technological knowledge. By use of angelic energy they achieve a perfect mode of living: educating, helping, and healing those in need.

Spiritual people use the angelic power as a path of discovery for different purposes. They use this power in the knowledge that it is special grant from God. He gives them a sacred and noble trust that has the potential to govern countless bodies other than their own. This ability is defined as "the angelic power in them." These spiritual people are known in Islamic spirituality as *abdal*: "changed ones." They can move from one place to another in the blink of an eye. They can live at one and the same time in the first and the second place. They can live in many other places as well and yet

[97] Surat an-Naba, 78:37-38

maintain the same appearance as their original self. This is called ubiquity. Famous *abdal* in Sufi history are al-Junayd, Abd al-Qadir Jilani, Jalal al-Din Rumi, Muhyiddin ibn Arabi, Mansur al-Hallaj.

Sufi scholar-saints such as these, also known as knower-saints or gnostics (*ʿarif*, pl. *ʿarifun*), have confirmed that there is another world between that of human bodies on earth and that of angels, and have called that world the imaginal world. This imaginal world is more subtle than the earthly world and yet denser than the angelic world. This characteristic of the imaginal world allows the *abdal* to travel within that dimension in the way that we have mentioned.

The method used by these spiritual people can be described as a self-riddance of the trappings of gravity. Everything yearns for its origin and the body yearns for earth which is pulled by gravity. The spirit, however, yearns to the heavenly realm which pulls upwards. These *abdal* were capable of balancing the opposite elements earth/heaven, or upward/downward, within themselves in such a way that the element earth which once dominated over the other is now dominated by the other and follows it.

The intellect dominates the conscience to the extent that some have said that the conscience is in the prison of the mind. If the intellect is of the destructive type, that person will use knowledge and self-discovery to hurt instead of to heal. Laser beams can be used for destruction as well as healing, but they are the same rays in either case. If that intellect does not balance properly between right and wrong, then it will be using the knowledge it acquires in an inappropriate way. If, however, the conscience dominates and plays a greater role, it will at one point dominate over the mind and ensure that it is controlled by the yearning to do good. That is best for himself and for humanity at large, for that person will be constantly motivated to use his knowledge to help and to serve others.

This is the case in the body that imprisons the spirit: the person who can balance the two poles within will be qualified as a

wise one. Further down the road, if that person can progress more in the heavenly direction, he can use his spirit to dominate the body and acquire those powers that cut through the fetters of gravity. This enables him to use the spirit to move the mass of the body, not only his own but those of others as well. For such a spirit, when it connects with its angelic power, will become a form of energy and light. These entities can move mass at higher speeds than the mind can conceive.

This is how these pious people known as saints or *abdal* were known to appear at any critical time and any place that they liked. Thus, they help people and teach them. The ubiquitous appearances of one's person in many places are like reflected images of the same one body through the mirror of an angelic power. This mirror produces thousands upon thousands of pictures at the same time, except that those pictures are every bit as real as the original which is being reflected.

God will create an angel called al-Natiq, "the Uttering Angel," out of His own dhikr (remembrance) of Himself for every one of these types of realized people. That angel is instructed to inhabit the heart of the pious servant of God. His duty is to continuously inform that servant of his duties and obligations in each twenty-four hour cycle, besides the known duties of worship. This link of information establishes a further possibility for the saint of reaching other human beings through the power of his heart.

Furthermore, God will enable him to hear the minutest cell in his body. The angel speaks to him and explains why God created it, what physical purpose it serves in the body, what can poison it, and what can heal it. Moreover, it will inform him how to heal himself from any disorder of his body, and enable him to heal others through his acquired angelic energy.

The saint's angelic power thus enables him to converse freely with every cell in his body as if he were speaking to another person sitting in the same room. This ability will open for him the understanding that the human body to which is joined an angelic power is greater and even less fathomable than this entire universe. Indeed, each cell is a world unto itself. It is inhabited by all kinds of infinitesimally small spiritual laborers. Their function is to run the life support system of that cell. A factory needs all kinds of instruments and machines, labor and managers to keep it alive and protect it from any kind of error and destruction. In the same way, scientifically speaking, the cell has its own defense system against any invader from outside: that protection is produced by the tiny angelic staff whom God created for that purpose.

As the saint becomes more and more perceptive in his inner hearing and speaking, he will concentrate his entire power. He then places it in his heart exclusively of any other focal point. This process can be compared to the concentration of light which does not burn if scattered over the paper, but burns if reassembled into one ray under a magnifying glass. At that time the saint will be able to send that gathered angelic light out of his heart in order to reach any human being on this earth and any heavenly being above.

The continuous build-up of this angelic power in the saint's heart allows him to witness heavenly sights and acquire heavenly knowledge. This continues until the day comes when an indescribable light appears in the horizon of his heart. This light expands the heart to an infinitesimal degree. It removes from it all the remaining veils that up to this point prevented it from reaching the realities of the heavenly world. Meanwhile, God orders the angels, each one in his state, duty, and position, to inform that pious individual of three things: the reason of his creation, his position in the divine scheme, and his duty within creation. Every single one of these angels will thereupon adorn that pious person. They will endow him with a kind of gift. At a certain point, he will himself become "dilated" which, in the language of mystics, means that he will be clad in a subtle body of light, the same light that characterizes angelic beings. That body is not visibly transparent to other human beings. Nevertheless, they can feel the light that emanates from the saint's body and be attracted to him as a magnet attracts other elements.

When people are attracted to this Knower-saint, however, he must not show that he is different from others and pretend to be higher than them. He must be an instrument of this angelic power. Being proud puts him in the same category as Satan. Although the latter possessed an angelic power he fell from heaven because of pride and that power was taken away from him. The saint must only use angelic power in a constructive way, for the happiness and benefit of human beings. He must do so without asking for anything in return from those he helps. Angels never ask anything for themselves, rather, they always ask for the sake of human beings.

Children have not been involved in the low desires that strip the heart of its angelic power. In fact, they are at the rank of saints although they themselves are unaware of it, much less their parents and relatives. The child that declares that he has visions and sights is telling the truth; whereas the parent who hears the child's accounts sifts them through the grid of the mind and does not consider them factual. "I heard music," "an angel came to me," "people came and disappeared," "they brought me gifts," are frequent utterances of children who blurt out these statements as the event occurs. The child cannot control himself; however, the saint keeps all these events hidden from others.

An intermediary state of knowledge exists between that of children and knower-saints which may be called a "premature sainthood." In that state many people experience visitations and sights and sounds which may be few and far in-between, or on the contrary frequent. These happenings seem discontinuous and even perhaps incoherent, like someone being addressed in a foreign language and struggling to understand. The reason is that those experiencing them have not achieved the state of purity that permits them to converse fluently with their angelic power. Like children, they cannot help revealing these experiences as soon as they occur or shortly thereafter in ways that may or may not make sense to them or to others.

The happiness that these retellers of angelic visitations feel in telling others of their experiences is like the happiness of a child who receives candy. A child will become happy with its candy and forget about a diamond. Nevertheless the goal remains the diamond. It is important for persons to always re-direct themselves towards that goal: the continuous connection of their heart with angelic power at every moment of their life.

Each human spirit evolves from the point when it was present and testified before God on the Day of promises, to the reality of earthly life then to the life of the grave then to eternal life. This evolution consists in changes from one image to another. The garment the spirit takes in the fourth month of its life in the womb is kept until death. Another dress is put on in the grave, which also deteriorates. Finally, the spirit puts on the body of the hereafter. This body changes to an angelic body at the time it enters among the angels, as we have already mentioned in relation to the Quranic verse:

*Enter thou My servants.*[98]

That angelic body will keep on changing, continuously and forever, from one excellent dress to one even more excellent, according to God's infinite creation of the levels of Paradise. Each dress of paradise, when worn, opens a new level. When one sees this new level, he desires to attain it. He puts on this new garment by divine permission. And a resurrection from one level of Paradise to the next continues ad infinitum. This astonishing phenomenon shows the great extent of God's power of creation.

In every period of evolution from one dress to another prior to Paradise the individual can understand his surroundings and in what state he is. He will be living in that very state and experiencing it but he cannot understand the other states. A person is virtually imprisoned in the state he is in and cannot see any other state. On the other hand, the individual who reaches the full state of sainthood

[98] Surat al-Fajr, 89:29

can understand everything from beginning to end. That is what differentiates the ordinary individual from the saint. A saint has already acquired the subtle body of light which enables him to see the past, present and future in one brief moment. Indeed, he can attain the knowledge of the souls from the moment they stood in the divine presence to the day they came to this world, entered the grave, were resurrected and stood before God again, and entered Paradise. This reality is expressed in the following prophetic tradition in which one of the Companions of the Prophet was asked by the latter to give those present a glimpse of his angelic vision:

> Harith ibn Laʿman said: "Once I went to the Prophet and he asked me in what state I spent the day. I replied: "As a true believer." Then the Prophet asked me the state of my faith. I replied: "I see the Throne of God and the people of Paradise helping each other, and the people of hell lamenting in hell. I see in front of me eight heavens and seven hells as clear as idol-worshipers see their idols. I can recognize each individual just like a miller can recognize wheat from barley. That is, who is to go to Paradise, and who is to be found in Hell. In front of me people are like fish and ants. Shall I stay silent or continue?" The Prophet told me to stop and say no more." [Imam Abu Hanifah, *al-Fiqh al-Akbar*].

One of these accomplished saints in more recent times said:

> I met an angel standing on the shore of a vast ocean. I saluted him, and the angel replied: "*Wa alaykum al-salam wa rahmat Allah.*" Then the angel asked me by my name, "O So-and-So, how is your shaykh, the master of *abdal*?" and he named him. I answered him by giving him good news about my shaykh, then I asked him how he knew him. He expressed surprise and answered: "Do you think we do not know him? Everyone in our realm knows and respects him.

When God elevated him to his rank He informed everyone in His creation, all the angels and every single creation on earth, that that person had reached the station where He loves him, and He wants everyone to love him also. Therefore, every stone, tree, animal, angel and jinn love him." I said: "There are some people on earth who want to kill him because they are jealous of his angelic knowledge and power." The angel said: "It is impossible that anyone can kill the one whom God loves and has raised to an angelic power."

The angel continued:

"Your master can hear and see the image of every created object in this universe. In this universe, there is nothing but these created reflections. They represent angels, human beings, and every element, living and non-living; and all of them are praising their Lord. All creation, except human beings who did not reach the state of angelic vision, are given a knowledge that enable them to hear each other's praising and hymning in whatever orbit of space or existence they move. Everyone praises his Lord with his own attributes and in the words of his own language. God gives everyone the understanding of the other's language but not the permission to use it. He has to use his own language."

I interrupted the angel: "Even the inanimate elements can understand the praising of others?"

"Yes, even they can understand. A stone is inanimate to human eyes but it is a living and praising creation. Haven't you heard of those who heard the stones praising God in the presence of the Prophet and his Companion-saints?'"

He continued: "We angels have been created out of divine light, and we have been greatly honored! Yet we both admire and pity you, human beings, because you have been created in God's image. Haven't you heard the saying of the Prophet: 'God created Adam after his likeness'? We understand this to mean that human beings have been elevated to a rank where He honored them by allowing them to reflect His image. This honor has raised human beings to a very high level. That is why God said in the Holy Quran:

> *Verily We have honored human beings, and We have carried them over the earth and over the sea.*[99]

These two bodies, earth and the ocean, here represent the external knowledge and the internal."

Such honoring of human beings is chiefly represented by their face, and the head is the true center of gravity of human beings. For you cannot say that the perfect place denoted by the word 'likeness,' in God's creation of human beings, consists in this or that limb of the body, as they are all the same from one person to another. But every one has a different face and there lies God's likeness. That is why the Prophet scolded the man who struck another on the face and forbade the striking of the face of human beings, even in battle."

When God wants to manifest Himself, He looks at His creation. His first attention goes to human beings because they resemble him. Those who resemble Him the most among them are the saints; hence the Prophet said of them: 'They remind you of God.' We

---

[99] Surat al-Isra, 17:70

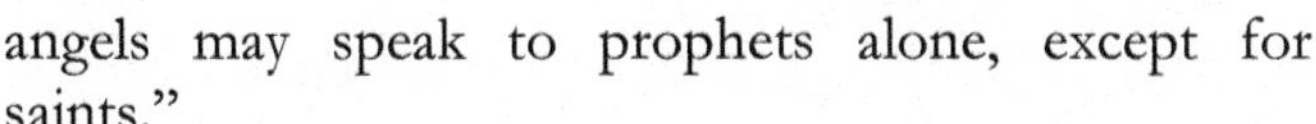



angels may speak to prophets alone, except for saints."

We also pity you because human beings are unwilling to open themselves to attract the angelic power by which they reach the state of heavenly knowledge that is their inheritance. That makes us appear in your human form in varying shapes and degrees of light, in different places and to different ages of human life, to remind you that you have been honored with an angelic power and a divine likeness. Keep the likeness! Use the angelic power! It shall elevate you to that luminous station without which God said:

> *Verily, those for whom God did not appoint light, they will never inherit light!*[100]

and He said: *'Light upon light!'*[101] declaring that the light of the heart's vision must be connected with the light of angelic power, ensuring success and guidance to all human beings. That light shall then appear over the entire human realm like a rising sun and a rising moon over all of creation, without ever setting. The light of this power, at that time, will make every individual like a moon, that is, a heavenly body that will reflect the original light for the rest of creation. By this light, this world will be preserved, the love of nature will rule the earth, and everyone will live in peace and love, swimming in the ocean of angelic beauty and harmony."

The angel spoke this; then he gave me the angelic greeting of peace and left.

---

[100] Surat an-Nur, 24:40

[101] Surat an-Nur, 24:35

# Sources

The principal sources for **Angels Unveiled** after the Quran are:

- The eight books of Authentic Traditions.

- al-Suyuti, **al-Haba'ik fi akhbar al-mala'ik.**

- Ibn Kathir, **Qisas al-anbiya.**

- al-Najjar, **Qisas al-anbiya.**

- al-Thaʿlabi, **Qisas al-anbiya.**

- al-Sufuri, **Nuzhat al-majalis wa muntakhab al-nafa'is.**

- al-Dayrini, **Taharat al-qulub wal-khuduʿ li ʿallam al- ghuyub.**

- al-Nabahani, **Jamiʿ Karamat al-awliya.**

- al-Isfahani, **Hilyat al-awliya.**

- Ibn ʿArabi, **al-Futuhat al-Makkiyya.**

- Ibn ʿArabi, **Tafsir al-Qur'an al-Karim.**

- Ms. of Shaykh Sharafuddin al-Daghestani, 38th Grandshaykh of the Naqshbandi Golden Chain, Private collection.

- Ms. of Shaykh Abdullah al-Daghestani, 39th Grandshaykh of the Naqshbandi Golden Chain, Private collection.

- Nasir al-Din's saying in the chapter entitled "the Angels of Mercy and Wrath" is adapted from William Chittick's translation in **Faith and Practice of Islam: Three Thirteenth-Century Sufi** Texts (Albany: SUNY Press, 1992) p. 78.

CPSIA information can be obtained
at www.ICGtesting.com
Printed in the USA
LVOW03s0004100817
544407LV00004B/468/P